THEODORA FITZGIBBON

A TASTE OF SCOTLAND

Scottish Traditional Food

Period photographs specially prepared by George Morrison

Pan Books London and Sydney

For Kitty Forbes,
with love and many thanks from us both

First published 1970 by J. M. Dent and Sons Ltd
This edition published 1971 by Pan Books Ltd,
Cavaye Place, London SW10 9PG
7th printing 1978
© Theodora FitzGibbon 1970
ISBN 0 330 02872 3
Printed in Great Britain by
Fletcher & Son Ltd, Norwich

ACKNOWLEDGEMENTS

wish to thank all the friends who have helped me in my research, articularly Miss Kitty Forbes for family papers, photographs and ooks, Sir John Forbes, Bart, and Lady Forbes, of Allargue, orgarff, Aberdeenshire, for the loan of family photographs; also r I. F. Grant for many of the remarkable photographs shown in is book.

My thanks are also due to the following people for their kindness nd help in the preparation of this book: Miss Dickson, Mrs Arm-rong and Mr C. S. Minto of the Central Public Library, Edin-urgh, for their valuable assistance; Miss Elspeth Yeo and Mr lervyn Lloyd of the National Library of Scotland, Edinburgh, oth of whom went to great trouble for me; Mr R. E. Hutchison nd Mr I. F. Hunter, of the National Portrait Gallery of Scotland; Ir Fenton and Mr John Baldwin of the National Museum of ntiquities of Scotland; Mr William Hood, Kirkcaldy Art Galleries; r D. M. Torbet, FLA, Central Public Library, Dundee; Mr orman Crawford, Arbroath Public Library; Miss Cruft and Mr Dunbar, MH, FSA, Ancient and Historical Monuments of Scotland; liss Moira Wilkie, FLA, Aberdeen Public Library, who supplied ot only photographs but also historical details; Mr Robert Blair Vilkie, Old Glasgow Museum, Glasgow, for his kindness and help; nd finally Mr Peter Leith of Stenness, Orkney, for his co-operation

and the kind loan of the late Mr William Hourston's (of Stromness, Orkney) photographs, pages 55 and 89.

Photographs on pages 3, 4, 7, 14, 31, 51, 61, 69, 70, 83, 84, 95, 100, 103, 105 are reproduced by kind permission of Dr I. F. Grant and the Central Public Library, Edinburgh: on pages 11, 22, 49, 67, 87, 90, 98, 107, 111, 116 by kind permission of the Central Public Library, Edinburgh. Photographs on pages 26, 37, 38, 40, 58, 76, 79 are reproduced by kind permission of the National Portrait Gallery, Edinburgh.

Photographs on pages 33, 64, 81, 119 from the George Washington Wilson Collection, by kind permission of the Aberdeen Central Public Library, Aberdeen.

Photographs on pages 72 and 97 from the Cathcart Collection, and 112 from the Curwen Collection, by kind permission of the National Museum of Antiquities of Scotland, Edinburgh.

Photograph on page 43 is reproduced by kind permission of The Royal Commission on the Ancient and Historical Monuments of Scotland, Edinburgh.

Photograph on page 45 is reproduced by kind permission of the Arbroath Public Library, Arbroath.

The photograph of Thomas Carlyle, page 62, by kind permission of Mr William Hood, Kirkcaldy Art Gallery and Museum.

Photograph on page 93, by kind permission of T. & R. Annan & Sons Ltd, Glasgow.

INTRODUCTION

All the Celtic countries – Scotland, Ireland, Wales and Brittany – have many things in common: a similarity of language; cultural heritages; as well as a surprising number of foods general to all those countries. There is little to choose between the Barm Brack of Ireland, the Bara Brith of Wales, Selkirk Bannock of Scotland, the Morlaix *Brioche* of Brittany, while the Buttery Rowies of Aberdeen are practically the same, apart from the shape, as the ordinary French breakfast *croissant*.

The girdle or griddle, one of the oldest cooking utensils in the world, plays a large part in the traditional dishes of them all, the name according to some authorities coming from the Old French *grédil*, meaning grid-iron, and to others, from the Gaelic word *greadeal*, the name for the hot stones used for baking by the early Gaels. It is not therefore surprising to find that girdle cakes in many forms exist from Ireland to Brittany. Indeed, the name of the Irish and Scottish girdle-baked potato cakes called Fadge, comes from the French *fouace*, meaning hearth, the hot hearth stones under the ashes being used to cook them.

The similarity does not end there, for all these countries make outstanding and original use of oatmeal, from the *Pain d'avoine* of Quimperlé, Brittany, the oatcakes of Scotland, Ireland and Wales, to the creamy oatmeal soup (*Potage crème d'avoine* in Brittany) of Scotland.

All these countries were also visited by the Vikings, and this, too, has led to Scandinavian methods of cooking, as well as salting and curing fish: the fish that have been the life's blood in all the countries' economic structures; not forgetting the prime Aberdeen Angus cattle, probably of Viking stock, also the salted and smoked mutton, which is still a speciality in Scotland and Scandinavian countries.

Scotland's ties with France begin as far back as Charlemagne in the ninth century, 'well keipt ancient alliance, maid betwix Scotland and the realme of France'. Many French queens with their courtiers have left their mark, not only in the kitchen but also in the language: the old French measure, *chopine*, is used frequently in many cookery books and manuscripts; *gigot* is common to both countries for a leg of lamb or mutton; ashet, for an oval, flat serving dish, from the French *assiette*; and many other words which will be found in this book. Those of my readers wishing to know more of Scotland's culinary history should consult Miss F. Marian McNeill's excellent and scholarly work, *The Scots Kitchen* (Blackie & Son Ltd, London and Glasgow, 1929 and 1963).

The excellence of Scottish food needs no boosting from me for many of her dishes have been absorbed into the *cuisine* of other English-speaking countries, as have the Welsh rarebit of Wales and the Irish stew of Ireland. She has contributed many original daily foods such as bitter-orange (Dundee) marmalade, porridge, kippers and smoked haddocks; the undisputed king of game birds, the grouse, not forgetting the two sauces, bread sauce and egg sauce, usually erroneously referred to as 'English'.

I make no apologies, as a foreigner, for writing about Scottish food: it is done from sincere appreciation, and admiration of her cooking, the cooking which has a long tradition yet is still to be found in that beautiful country, as are all the ingredients which are given here. I do, however, apologize for having to omit so many things, but this book is, both visually and literally 'a taste of Scotland'. I hope it will bring new ideas to some of my readers, as well as reviving happy memories for others; as the old Gaelic proverb says: ''S mairg a ni tarcuis air biadh' – 'Foolish is he that despises food'.

THEODORA FITZGIBBON, 197

Deilginis   Dalke
Baile Áth Cliath   Dubli

Some hae meat and cannot eat,
And some would eat that want it;
But we hae meat, and we can eat,
Sae let the Lord be thankit.

Robert Burns, 1759–96,
'Grace before Meat'

DUNDEE CAKE

the last century a sweet bannock made from oatmeal and sugar, then
*mixed with cream and cooked in a heavy pan, was served to the company
women present at a child's birth. This was called a 'cryin' bannock'.
The Reverend Walter Gregor in Notes on the Folklore of the North-
*East of Scotland, 1881, says that when the child first started to cut a
*tooth, a bannock of oatmeal, butter and cream, baked with a ring in it,
*was given to the child to play with; when it broke everyone present was
given a small piece and the child used the ring as a teething ring.

*Dundee cake makes an excellent christening, wedding or Christmas
cake which will keep for some months in a tin.

oz. (⅔ cup) butter

oz. (⅔ cup) sugar

small eggs

heaped tablesp. ground
almonds

oz. (1 cup) sultanas or seedless
raisins

oz. (1 cup) currants

oz. (1 cup, scant) chopped,
mixed peel

tablesp. milk having been
boiled, and cooked, with 1
tablesp. sugar

3 oz. (1 cup, scant) halved glacé
cherries

Grated rind and juice ½ lemon

8 oz. (2 cups) flour

1 level teasp. baking powder

1 tablesp. brandy or rum

1 oz. blanched split almonds

pinch of salt

METHOD OF PREPARING THE DRIED FRUITS
several hours prior to making the cake, which makes it impossible
for them to sink to the bottom, and brings out the flavour and juices:
put the glacé cherries, sultanas, currants and peel into a casserole,
and mix them thoroughly with the hands, cover with a lid or foil and
put into a slow oven (220–240° F.) until it is well heated through,
stirring it at least once with a fork, for about 20 minutes, or until it
is sticky. Take it out, and let it get completely cold before using.
Rolling dried fruit in flour makes the cake hard, and washing has the
same effect.

Cream the butter well, work in the sugar, and when white and creamy
add the eggs one at a time alternately with a good sprinkle of flour,
beating well all the time. Stir in the ground almonds, and add the
dried fruits, peel and the lemon rind and juice, also a pinch of salt.
Mix the remaining flour with the baking powder, mix it into the
mixture, and finally stir in the brandy or rum. Turn into an 8-in.
cake tin that has been greased and lined with greased paper. Cover
with foil and bake in a slow to moderate oven (300° F.) for about
2½ hours. Half-way through cooking time remove the paper and
scatter the split almonds on top. Test with a skewer before removing
from the oven, and 5 minutes before it is ready brush over the top
with the sweetened milk, then put it back to give it a nice glaze when
it is dry. Do not remove from the tin until it is cold.

Christening party in the Highlands, c. 1860

R EDWARE, SLOKE, DULSE

'Our exquisite fragile and delicate Forms
Are reared by the Ocean, and rocked by the Storms'.

Anon.

The seaweeds most eaten in Scotland are redware (Porphyra lacinata), also known as sea-tangle or tangle, which is similar to Sloke (P. vulgaris), sea-spinach; Dulse (Rhodymenia palmata) which is a reddish-brown colour, and Carrageen (Chondrus crispus). The last two can be found in a prepared form in most health-food shops.

In the old days, children on the Scottish islands would eat stalks of redware raw, or roasted over peat embers and then put on to a buttered bannock. All seaweeds are rich in minerals, and form the basis for good soups or a sauce with roast lamb, or may be stewed and served with mashed potatoes.

If the seaweed is gathered freshly it must be very well washed in running water to remove all sand. Then soak it in cold water for 2 hours, and strain. Simmer it gently in water to cover, with a lid on, for at least 3 or 4 hours (for such a lacy, delicate-looking plant, it takes a remarkably long time to cook), then drain. It is well beaten with pepper and salt to taste, a knob of butter, and finished with good squeeze of lemon and orange juice. When cooked for the correct time it becomes a soft jelly. The taste is extremely delicate like a very mild jelly flavoured with anchovy.

When cooked, it can also be mixed with a little oatmeal, shaped into small, flat cakes, and fried for breakfast.

SEAWEED SOUP

1 cup cooked sloke or dulse	½ lb. (2 cups) mashed potatoes
3 pt. (6 cups) milk	1 tablesp. butter (melted)
juice of 1 lemon	pepper

Simmer the milk, cooked seaweed and potato together for about minutes, then either beat well or liquidize. Season to taste, add the melted butter and the lemon juice, and beat again. Heat up and serve hot.

Serves 6.

Cutting redware or sea-tangle, Skye, c. 18

WHOLEMEAL BREAD

Makes 2 loaves

2 lb. (8 cups) wholemeal flour	1 oz. yeast
1 lb. (4 cups) white flour	1 teasp. salt
2 oz. (¼ cup) melted butter	¼ pt. (½ cup) tepid water
½ pt. (1 cup) tepid milk	a pinch of sugar

See that the mixing basin is slightly warm, then put in the sifted flours and mix them together well, then add the butter. Cream the yeast with the sugar and add the tepid water and milk. Make a well in the flour and pour in the liquid. Using a wooden spoon mix to a smooth dough, adding the salt gradually. Cover with a cloth and leave in a warm place until double the size (about 1 hour). Take out from the bowl and knead well on a floured board or table until it is soft and not sticky. Divide into two, and shape into loaves, then put into greased tins (this is not essential if a round or 'cottage' loaf is liked), the dough coming to about ⅔ of the way up. Cover, and leave again in a warm place for about ¾ hour, or until the dough is nearly to the top of the pans. Bake in a moderate to hot oven (400° F.) for 10 minutes, then lower the heat to 350° F. and continue cooking for about 35 minutes. The loaf will sound hollow when tapped on the bottom, if properly cooked.

For white bread use 1½ lb. (6 cups) white flour, and ½ pt. (1 cup) mixed tepid milk and water.

Grinding corn by quern, and spinning, Orkneys, c. 1890

MINCED COLLOPS

Collop is possibly from the French *escalope*; it can also mean veal, or small slices of any meat.

'By five or six he was up, having his "morning" – a glass of ale or brandy, over which he reverently said a grace, which was brief when he was alone, longer when he was in company, before he visited his "policy" and stables and fields. When breakfast was served at eight o'clock he was ready for the substantial fare of skink [an old Scots stew-soup] *or water gruel, supplemented by collops, or mutton aided with ale. The bread consisted of oatmeal cakes or barley bannocks.'*
The Social Life of Scotland in the 18th century,
Henry Gray Graham, 1899.

A hundred years later, the fare was very similar, and even today, the same dishes are found all over Scotland.

1 lb. minced steak	1 tablesp. oatmeal
½ pt. (1 cup) stock (½ stock cube dissolved will do)	2 small finely chopped onions
1 tablesp. mushroom relish, ketchup or Worcestershire sauce	1 tablesp. butter or oil
	salt and pepper

Heat the fat in a shallow saucepan, and when hot add the onions, and fry gently until lightly coloured. Then add the steak, and fry it until brown on all sides. Season to taste and stir in the oatmeal which gives it an agreeable nutty taste, then add the stock. Cover and simmer very gently for about ½ hour, then flavour with the mushroom relish to taste. Serve either with triangles of toast, or with a border of mashed potatoes. It can also be garnished with slices of hard-boiled eggs or served with poached eggs.

Hare, venison or other game can be used, seasoned with allspice; half port wine and half stock is used.

SCOTCH COLLOPS

Adapted from Cookery and Pastry as taught and practised by Mrs Maciver, Teacher of those Arts in Edinburgh, *1783–97.*

Take thin veal slices from the thigh, and beat them well, then brown in butter; add a mutchkin (½ pt.) stock, ½ lemon peel, grated, a pinch of mace, 3 tablespoons wine, and simmer gently for 20 minutes. Thicken with a *beurre manié* (nut of butter rolled in flour), add pickled oysters or mushrooms. Finally beat 1 egg yolk with 2 tablespoons cream, salt and a pinch of nutmeg, stir in, heat up, but do not reboil.

Woodcutting in the Highlands, c. 1890

PINEAPPLE WATER ICE

Also for peach, apricot, strawberry, marmalade etc.; from The Complete Confectioner and Family Cook, *John Caird, 1809.*

'We got a fair dinner at the village inn, and a splendid desert [sic] *of peaches from the mansion house.'* (Gartmore).
Tour in the Hebrides, *George L. A. Douglas, Advocate, Sheriff of the Shire of Kincardine, 1800.*

1 lb. (2 cups) pineapple jam   juice of 2 lemons
¾ pt. (1½ cups) water   4 oz. (½ cup, scant) sugar
1 egg white stiffly beaten
  (optional)

Boil the sugar and water together for 10 minutes, then add the lemon juice. Mix well with the jam, and either sieve or liquidize for 1 minute. Put into the ice-tray and freeze until it is slushy but not firm. Then remove and either liquidize or beat well with a rotary beater, and if using the egg white, stir it in well. Put back into the tray and freeze again until firm.
    Serves 4–6.

By a waterfall in the Trossachs, c. 18

MUSSEL AND ONION STEW

Musselburgh, with its Roman bridge across the Esk, was once the site of a Roman camp, and owes its name to the famous mussel bed found at the mouth of the river. It has always been a great mussel-eating centre, and the following recipe comes from near by: the Open Arms, Dirleton, East Lothian.

Oysters, scallops, clams, cockles or other molluscs or bivalves can be cooked in the same way.

60 mussels (about 2–3 qt.)	½ bottle white wine
2 large onions	½ pt. (1 cup) cream
2 heaped tablesp. butter	2 tablesp. chopped parsley
2 heaped tablesp. flour	salt and pepper
1 pt. (2 cups) warm milk	

Wash and scrub the mussels well, and discard any that are open. Put them through several waters to remove the sand and grit. Then place them, unopened, into a large saucepan, add the wine, put a lid on and bring to the boil. Let them simmer gently for about 10 minutes until they are all open. Then strain off the liquid and reserve it. Meanwhile take the mussels from the shells, removing the beards. Melt the butter in a saucepan, stir in the flour, then add the mussel liquor, stirring all the time, followed by the warm milk. Stir frequently so that it does not go into lumps. Add the onion, finely chopped, and simmer gently until cooked. Season to taste, add t[...] parsley, mussels and cream, bringing it gently to just under boilin[...] point. Serve at once, in warmed soup plates. If the mussels a[...] allowed to boil they can become rubbery.

Serves 4–6.

MUSSEL BROSE

Traditional.

60 mussels	½ pt. (1 cup) water
1 pt. (2 cups) milk	2 heaped tablesp. fine oatmeal
salt and pepper	

Wash the mussels as above, and put into a large saucepan with t[...] water, cover, and heat until they open. Strain the liquor into a bas[...] and shell and beard the mussels. Lightly toast the oatmeal a[...] reserve. Then heat up the milk with the mussel juice, season [...] taste, and add the mussels, but do not let them boil. Put the oatme[...] in a large bowl, and add ½ pt. (1 cup) of the boiling stock, stirring quickly so that it forms knots like small dumplings. Add to the so[...] and serve hot.

Serves 4–6.

baker's cart, Musselburgh, 1886. Photograph by Mr Aird

TROUT FRIED IN OATMEAL

'The situation of Dalmally is truly beautiful on the banks of Loch Awe, and commanding a view of the fine old castle of Kilchurn, belonging to the Earl of Breadalbane . . . we got a very good dinner, as well as wine, and were joined by some very smart tourists at that meal, whose destination seemed to be the same as our own.' 31st July, 1800.
Tour in the Hebrides, *George L. A. Douglas.*

In the 1780s Faujas de Saint-Fond, the King of France's Commissioner for wines, said of the inn at Dalmally: 'We were astonished at its elegance in so desert a place . . . our supper consisted of two dishes of fine game, the one of heathcock [blackcock, Lyruris tetrix], the other of woodcock, a creamy fresh butter, cheese of the country, a pot of Vaccinium [blaeberries], a wild fruit which grows on the mountains, and port wine – all served up together. It was truly a luxurious repast for the country.'

There is still a very good hotel at Portsonachan, by Dalmally, Argyll, and fresh, fried Loch Awe trout is one of their specialities.

Allow 1 large trout or 2 small ones per person. Clean the trout and split them open at the belly, then remove the backbone. Season some coarse oatmeal with salt and pepper, then roll the fish on both sides in it. Heat 2 tablespoons butter for each 2 fish, in a frying-pan, and when bubbling, but not brown, fry the fish on both sides until golden. Drain, and serve garnished with parsley and wedges of lemon.

This recipe is also used for herrings.

Boating on Loch Awe, 186

POTATO SCONES

½ lb. (2 cups) boiled mashed potatoes

2½ oz. (⅔ cup) flour

3 tablesp. melted butter or bacon fat

½ teasp. salt

Mash the potatoes well, and add the melted fat and salt, then add as much flour as the potatoes will take without becoming too dry. (This amount varies with the kind of potato used: the floury kind will need less than the others.) Turn out on to a floured board and roll until ¼ in. in thickness, then cut into circles, and then into farls or quarters. Prick all over with a fork, and cook, either on a fairly hot girdle, turning once, or in a heavy pan. If using the latter it should be wiped over with a greased paper before cooking starts. Makes approximately 3 large cakes or 12 farls.

They are served with butter, honey or syrup, and are sometimes rolled up when hot, and eaten the same day they are made.

CHEESE POTATO CAKES

To the above mixture add 4 oz. (1 cup) grated cheese, and 2 well-beaten eggs. Shape into little round cakes, dip in breadcrumbs and fry in ¼ in. of hot oil on both sides until golden. They are good as a supper or picnic dish.

This amount makes about 12 cakes.

rofter making a 'kashie' to carry peat, Zetland, Shetland Isles c. 1890

OATMEAL SOUP

This soup has a complex flavour, and is very creamy.

2 level tablesp. medium oatmeal
½ pt. (1 cup) milk
¼ pt. (½ cup) cream
1 tablesp. chopped parsley for garnish
salt and pepper

1 large onion
1 pt. (2 cups) chicken stock (a dissolved stock cube is adequate)
1 tablesp. butter or margarine

Melt the fat in a saucepan, chop the peeled onion finely and cook until soft but not brown, then add the oatmeal and seasonings, and cook for a few minutes. Add the stock, slowly, stirring all the time, bring to the boil, and simmer, covered, for ½ hour. Then either put through a sieve, or liquidize for 1 minute. Return to pan, reheat with the milk, and serve with cream and chopped parsley as garnish.

Serves 4–6.

Toasted oatmeal is used in many ways in Scotland: it is very good lightly toasted and mixed with vanilla ice-cream, which is the refrozen. Use 1 heaped tablespoon oatmeal to ½ lb. ice-cream. gives an agreeable, nutty, almost praline, flavour to the ice-cream.

CRANACHAN

This is a cream crowdie, made from toasting 2 heaped tablespoon oatmeal lightly, then mixing it into ½ pt. (1 cup) cream which ha been whipped until frothy, but not stiff, and sweetened to taste. can be flavoured with rum, vanilla (vanilla sugar can be used f sweetening) or 1 cup fresh raspberries (or other soft fruit), an makes an excellent dessert. Vanilla ice-cream can be used instead cream.

Serves 4.

The young Laird, Newe, Strathdon, Aberdeenshire, c. 19(

WILD DUCK WITH PORT WINE SAUCE

This recipe can also be used for widgeon or teal, but as they are smaller, they will only need half the cooking time.

2 wild ducks
juice of 1 lemon
4 rashers streaky bacon
1 teasp. mushroom relish or mushroom ketchup (optional)
2 tablesp. butter or oil

8 tablesp. port wine
2 level tablesp. orange marmalade
salt, cayenne pepper, and black pepper

Wild duck should be hung for about a week before cooking, if cold weather; three days if warmer, when a greenish tinge on the thin skin of the belly will be seen.

Cover the breasts with the bacon and put into a roasting tin with the fat or oil, then cook in a moderate oven (350° F.) for about 35 minutes. Before serving, the bacon should be removed (it can be used as a garnish) and the breasts scored along the breastbone, two or three times, then sprinkled with salt and pepper. Pour the port wine and the lemon juice over, and put them back in the oven for 5 minutes. Put the birds on to a warmed dish and reduce the pan juices on top of the stove with the marmalade, and mushroom relish added. If liked the birds can be flambéed by having 2 tablespoons warmed brandy poured over them, and then set alight. This should be done at the table. The gravy is served separately.

Serves 4–6.

Duck shooting, Loch Leven, c. 187

PETTICOAT TAILS

This name may be a corruption of the French petites gatelles, *little cakes, but in* Annals of the Cleikum Club *(incorporated in Meg Dods's* The Cook and Housewife's Manual) *1826, it says:* 'It may be so: in *Scottish culinary terms there are many corruptions, though we rather think the name petticoat tails has its origin in the shape of the cakes, which is exactly that of the bell-hoop petticoats of our ancient Court ladies.'*

The present-day makers of these crisp little biscuit-like cakes attribute them to Mary Queen of Scots, c. 1560, who was said to be very fond of them.

12 oz. (3 cups) sifted flour
6 oz. (⅔ cup) butter
3 heaped tablesp. caster sugar
½ gill (4 tablesp.) milk

2 teasp. caraway seeds (these are optional, only used in some parts of Scotland)

Mix the caraway seeds, if you are using them, with the flour, and melt the butter in the milk. Make a well in the centre of the flour, pour in the liquid, then add the sugar. Mix very well, and knead a little, but not too much, to get it thoroughly amalgamated. Put it on to a lightly floured board and roll out to ¼ in. thickness. Put an inverted dinner plate on top and cut around the edges. Remove the plate and cut a small round around the middle with a wine glass.

Keep this inner circle whole, but cut what is remaining into 8 segments, not cutting right through the paste, but making a deep incision. Bake on a greased paper laid on a flat sheet in a moderate oven (350° F.) for about 20 minutes, or until crisp and golden. Cool on a wire rack, dust with caster sugar, and serve with the round cake in the middle, and the 'petticoat tails' around it.

Sketching near St Boswell's, Roxburghshire, 1858

MUTTON-HAMS

...well-known Scottish speciality, and in many places, particularly ...ithness, geese are still cured and smoked, as well as joints of beef. ... the eighteenth century the Scottish border was famous for these ...ams' and many were exported from Glasgow to the West Indies and ...e New World.

...O CURE A LEG OF MUTTON LIKE ...AM

...dapted from an eighteenth-century manuscript.

...gigot of leg of mutton, about ...10 lb.	1 lb. dark brown sugar
...pt. water	2 oz. Jamaica pepper (allspice)
...lb. coarse salt, preferably sea-...salt	1 oz. peppercorns
...oz. saltpetre	1 tablesp. coriander seeds
	8 crushed juniper berries

...his brine can also be used for beef, pork, duck or goose).

Boil all the ingredients for 5 minutes, then leave to cool. Strain into a deep, clean bucket or crock, and completely immerse the meat or bird in it. Keep covered in a dry place at a temperature of under 60° F. Beef, mutton and pork should be left for between 10 and 14 days depending on size of the joints; duck and geese (both with giblets removed) should lie for 2 days for a duck and 4 days for a large goose. When removed from the brine, the joint should be washed, and soaked for 4 hours.

For smoking, the joint should be hung over a fire of either peat or hard wood with a juniper branch or berries smouldering in the embers, for 10 to 14 days; or it may be sent out to be smoked. All the meats or birds are excellent to eat without smoking.

Boiling time is 30 minutes to the pound, and cold water to cover the meat is essential, for hot water seals in the salt; any root vegetables can be added to the pot, and a teaspoon of dry mustard powder added to the water keeps the meat moist. If serving cold, leave the meat or bird to get cold in the stock. When serving hot the following accompaniments are served: with salt beef, pork or mutton – kail boiled, strained, chopped, seasoned and mixed with butter, called Lang Kail; mutton is also served with caper sauce (*see* page 106), duck and goose with onion sauce which is made like caper sauce, using 1 large sliced onion instead of capers.

SCOTS EGGS

Also called Scotch Eggs, are served for breakfast, or as a savoury, but also make a very useful picnic dish served with a salad.

10 eggs (8 hard-boiled)
1½ lb. pork sausage-meat
a pinch of mace
salt and pepper

4 oz. (1 cup) approx. breadcrumbs (crisp)
deep oil for frying

Boil 8 of the eggs for 10 minutes in boiling water, then drain and let them run under the cold tap, and when cool, shell them. Beat up one of the remaining eggs and add 1 tablespoon cold water. Season the sausage-meat and add the mace, then dip the hard-boiled eggs into the beaten egg, and cover each one entirely with the sausage-meat, pressing it on with the hands. Beat up the remaining egg and gently roll them in this, then dip them in the breadcrumbs (you may need slightly more than the amount given, depending on the size of the eggs) again pressing the breadcrumbs into the sausage-meat. Have the oil good and hot and fry them singly until the outside is golden brown. Lift up with the basket, and drain well before serving either hot with mustard, or cold with a chopped raw apple and celery salad dressed with 3 tablespoons olive oil to 1 of wine vinegar.

    Serves 4.

The Minister pays for his ponies, Ross and Cromarty, c. 18

STOVED CHICKEN

lso called Chicken Stovies, from the French *étouffée*, to stew in a osed vessel: a popular Highland dish which preserves all the essence the bird.

hickens figure very early on in Scottish literature, and hens were kept l over the country. In some of the low-country districts the keeping of wls was a condition of farm tenancy, the Laird taking eggs and ultry.

young chicken about 3 lb. cut into serving pieces	2 oz. (2 heaped tablesp.) butter
large sliced onions, or preferably 12 small, whole shallots	1 pt. (2 cups) stock made from the boiled giblets
lb. old potatoes, sliced medium thick in rounds	salt and pepper
	3 tablesp. chopped parsley as garnish (optional)

Melt 1 oz. of the butter in a saucepan and lightly brown the chicken joints on both sides in it, then remove the joints. Place a thick layer of sliced potatoes, then sliced onion or whole shallots, all well seasoned, on the bottom, then a layer of chicken, dotting each layer with little knobs of the remaining butter. Continue until all the food is finished, ending with a layer of potatoes. Pour over the stock, and cover first with a piece of buttered greaseproof paper, and then with the lid. Either simmer, or cook in a slow oven (275° F.) for about 2½ hours, adding a little more hot stock or water at half cooking time, if the liquid appears to have dried up too much. Sprinkle generously with the chopped parsley 5 minutes before serving.

Serves 4.

COCK-A-LEEKIE

Recipe of Rosa Mattravers, cook to Theodora, Lady Forbes, Newe, Strathdon, Aberdeenshire, for twenty-one years.

Cock-a-Leekie, one of the most famous Scots dishes, is more of a stew than a soup. Fynes Morrison writing in 1598 describes something very like it, eaten at dinner in a Knight's house: '. . . but the upper messe, insteede of Porredge, had a Pullet with some prunes in the broth'. The French diplomatist, Talleyrand, renowned for his gastronomic knowledge, thought that the prunes should be cooked with the soup, but removed before serving. Alexis Soyer, the famous chef, said: 'I will always give the preference in the way of soup to their Cock-a-Leekie, even before their inimitable Hotch-Potch!'

'Such were the cock-a-leekie and the savoury minced collops, which rivalled in their way even the veal cutlets of our old friend Mrs Hall at Ferrybridge.'

St Ronan's Well, *Sir Walter Scott.*

1 boiling fowl[1]	water to cover
a large veal or beef marrow bone (optional)	12 leeks
3 chopped rashers bacon	¼ lb. (1 cup) cooked prunes
salt and pepper	a mixed bunch of parsley, thyme and a bay leaf

Put the chopped bones, chicken, herbs, bacon, and all the leeks (chopped) except two, into a large saucepan with water to well cover. Put the lid on and let it simmer for 2 to 3 hours, until the bird is cooked. Top up with more water if necessary, but do not weaken it with too much. Season to taste, then strain, picking out the chicken and cutting it into serving pieces, also spooning out the marrow bones. Add these to the soup, together with the stoned prunes, and the remaining chopped leeks, then simmer very gently for not more than 15 minutes.

[1] If a whole bird is used it is enough for 6 or 8 people, but it can also be made with the carcase, and leg or wing joints of the bird.

SHRIMP OR PRAWN PASTE

An old family recipe. The paste was always served in a white soufflé dish, usually included in a cold buffet, or served with crisp toast for tea on special occasions.

> *'The traveller dines on potted meats,*
> *On potted meats and princely wine*
> *Not wisely but too well he dines,*
> *And breathing forth a pious wish*
> *He fills his belly full of fish.'*
>
> Robert Louis Stevenson

---

1 lb. cooked shrimps or prawns (approx. 2 cups, shelled)
¾ lb. (1½ cups) butter
1 lb. filleted haddock or other white fish
1 teasp. anchovy essence or 3 filleted anchovies
a pinch mace
a pinch cayenne pepper

Shell the cooked shrimps, and put the washed shells on to boil in enough water to barely cover them for ½ hour. Strain the liquid, and then poach the skinned haddock in it until it is cooked, about 10 minutes. (If the shrimps are already shelled when bought, poach the fish in water.) Drain the fish, leaving just a trace of liquid, and pound it to a paste with the mace, anchovy and cayenne to taste. Let it get quite cold. Now add all but 2 level tablespoons of the butter and beat until smooth. Add the chopped shrimps, heat together, but do not cook it, then press it into a deep dish about 6 in. in diameter and 3 in. high. When cool, melt the rest of the butter and pour over the top, then let it get quite cold. When cut it is a soft pink butter profusely studded with shrimps.

Serves 6.

iting the long-line, 1879

BUTTERY ROWIES

Traditional Aberdeen butter yeast rolls.

All utensils should be warm before starting.

1 lb. flour	8 oz. (1 cup) butter
1 oz. yeast or ½ tablesp. dried yeast	4 oz. (½ cup) lard
	¾ pt. (1½ cups) tepid water
1 tablesp. sugar	a pinch of salt

Mix the sifted flour and salt into a basin, then cream the yeast with the sugar. When it has bubbled up add it to the flour with the water, which must be blood heat only. Mix well, cover and set in a warm place until double the bulk, about ½ hour. Cream the butter and lard together and then divide into three. Put the dough on to a floured board and roll out into a long strip. Put the first third of fats in dots on to the top third of the pastry strip and fold over like an envelope, as if making flaky pastry. Roll out, and do this twice more until all the butter mixture is used up. Then roll out and cut into small oval shapes (or small rounds). Put on to a floured baking sheet with at least 2 in. between each one to allow for spreading. Cover, as above, and leave to rise for ¾ hour, then bake in a moderate to hot oven (375°–400° F.) for 20 minutes.

Makes about 15 (*see also* Baps, page 92).

CRULLAS

(*Traditional.*) *The name comes from the Gaelic* kril, *a small cake* bannock. *The American cruller from the Dutch* krullen, to curl, *is same sort of cake, which may have been introduced into Scotland fr Holland, and likewise Dutch settlers may have introduced them to United States.*

1 lb. (3½ cups) flour	4 oz. (½ cup) butter
1 teasp. bicarbonate of soda	4 oz. (½ cup) sugar
½ teasp. cream of tartar	4 eggs
½ teasp. salt	¼ pt. (½ cup) buttermilk or s milk
a pinch of nutmeg or ginger (optional)	deep oil for frying

Cream the butter and sugar, then add the eggs, flour, soda, nutm or ginger if used, cream of tartar and salt. Add the buttermilk slow mixing well, so that it becomes a firm dough (it may need sligh less or more buttermilk according to size of eggs). Put on to a flou board and roll into long strips. Cut into 1-in. ribbons leaving tops together, and plait them, damping the ends so they stick. H the oil very hot (365° F.), and fry until golden brown. Drain absorbent paper, and sprinkle with fine sugar.

Makes about 2 dozen.

Street scene, King Street, Aberdeen, c. 18

'Opening the hampers' – grouse drive at Edinglasse, 1882, with beaters and horses on the skyl

GROUSE

No fewer than four varieties of grouse exist in Scotland. The largest is the Capercaillie (Tetrao urogallus), a handsome bird with green, black, red and white plumage, also known as Cock o' the Woods. As it feeds on young pine shoots it must be cleaned soon after shooting, otherwise it has a faint turpentine flavour. There are also the Black Grouse (T. tetrix) known in France as Coq de Bruyère; the White Grouse or Ptarmigan (Lagopus mutus) which is brown and white in summer, and pure white in winter; and finally Red Scotch Grouse (L. scoticus) thought by gastronomes to be the finest game bird in the world. It exists only in Scotland and the very north of England in any quantity, although there are a very few in North Wales and Ireland.

Grouse should be hung for a week in warm weather and at least 10 days in cold. The young ones are usually roasted, the older birds being kept for casserole dishes, pies or pâtés. The young bird is easily recognizable by its clean claws with no noticeable moulting ridge, its soft breastbone tips, rounded spurs and downy feathers. From September to mid October is the best time to eat young grouse born the same year. They are so good that the simplest ways of cooking them are the best. Grouse is not usually stuffed, but in the Highlands the small wild mountain raspberries, rowan berries or wild cranberries are mixed with butter and put inside the birds. The fruit almost melts away during cooking, but the spicy, buttery juice seeps through.

2 young grouse
6 rashers fat bacon
1 gill (½ cup) port or claret
juice of 1 lemon or wild raspberries, etc.
½ lb. seeded, peeled white grapes
4 oz. (½ cup) butter
salt and pepper
sprigs of heather (if available) soaked in 2 tablesp. whisky

Wrap the birds in the bacon rashers and the whisky-soaked heather sprigs, and put a walnut-sized piece of butter mixed with a squeeze of lemon, salt and pepper (or the wild fruit if available) into the body of each bird before placing in the roasting pan. Add the rest of the butter to the pan and cook in a hot (400° F.) oven for 20 minutes. Then add the port or claret, baste well, and put back in the oven for 5 or 10 minutes. Remove the birds from the pan, take off the bacon and heather, and keep warm. Reduce the gravy on the top of the stove and serve separately. Serve the grouse with game chips, bread sauce if liked (*see* page 115) and a bowl of peeled and seeded white grapes in their own juice.

Serves 4.

Other accompaniments are: watercress, fried oatmeal or Skirlie (*see* page 80), fried breadcrumbs, rowan or cranberry jelly, or pickled peaches. This recipe can be used for pheasant (in which case allow 50–60 minutes cooking time), partridge, pigeon or guinea fowl.

SCOTS BROTH

Also Scotch or Barley Broth.

'. . . *You never ate it before?*' '*No sir,*' *replied Johnson,* '*but I don't care how soon I eat it again.*'
Journal of a Tour to the Hebrides, *1786, Boswell.*

2 lb. neck of mutton, trimmed of fat, and a knuckle bone if possible
3 oz. (3 heaped tablesp.) pot barley
3 oz. (1 cup) shelled peas, or ½ cup dried split peas according to season
1 large onion, sliced
white of 1 large leek
1 small cabbage
2 medium white turnips, diced
3 carrots, diced
2 tablesp. chopped parsley
5 pt. (10 cups) water
salt and pepper

Put the meat into a large saucepan with the water, bring to the boil, and then skim the top. Season to taste, then simmer gently for about 1 hour. Add the peas (if dried, add them with the meat to begin with), diced turnip, carrot, onion, leek, and the barley, cover and simmer for 20 minutes, then put in the shredded cabbage, and taste for seasoning. A few minutes before serving add the parsley. Serve hot, with one cutlet per person. Some cooks prefer to serve the broth first and then the meat afterwards with a caper sauce (*see* page 106). The vegetables can be varied according to what is in season, or to hand: kale instead of cabbage, celery, etc.

Serves about 8.

Garrison at Edinburgh Castle, c. 1847. Photograph by D. O. Hill

Roast Venison

Scotland is famous for the quality of its venison, and the finest is thought to come from animals which live up in the hills. Large joints should always be marinated before cooking.

haunch or saddle venison, about 6 lb.	salt and black pepper
tablesp. olive oil	2 tablesp. butter
	½ lb. diced salt pork or bacon

FOR THE MARINADE

bottle burgundy or claret	1 teasp. black peppercorns
cloves garlic	1 sprig rosemary
bay leaf	2 crushed juniper berries
carrots	4 tablesp. olive oil
large onion	

FOR THE SAUCE

pt. (½ cup) port wine	gravy from the venison
tablesp. redcurrant or rowan-berry jelly	1 tablesp. flour
	1 tablesp. butter

For the marinade, slice and peel the onion and carrots, then cook them gently in the olive oil, but do not let them brown. Put into a glass or earthenware dish (not metal), add the wine, and other ingredients. Soak the venison in this, for about 2 days, turning several times a day, so that all surfaces are coated with the marinade.

When it is ready, take it out and dry it with a clean cloth. Combine the butter and oil in a heavy pan that has a tight lid, and when hot add the diced pork or bacon. Fry until the cubes are crisp, then add the joint, and brown on all sides. Reduce the marinade to half by boiling it rapidly on top of the stove, and strain it over the venison. Season to taste, and cook in the oven at 325° F. for 30 minutes to the pound.

To make the sauce, strain off the pan juices, and reduce them again to half on top of the stove by boiling rapidly. Rub the flour into the butter, and add this to thicken it. Stir well, then add the port and redcurrant, or rowan, jelly, mixing it very well. Serve over the venison, or separately as desired. Braised celery, or a purée of chestnuts are traditionally served as accompaniments.

Left-over venison is excellent made into pasties (*see* page 73).

Dining-room at Mar Lodge, 1865

MELTING MOMENTS

'*During the old* régime, *the French moved from table to the ante-room to refresh their lips and fingers immediately after the substantial part of their repast. Madame the Comtesse de Genlis appears to consider the abandonment of this practice and the introduction of finger-glasses as one of the most flagrant innovations of* parvenu *manners.*'

The Cook and Housewife's Manual, *by Mistress Margaret Dods, of the Cleikum Inn, St Ronan's, 1826. Meg Dods was the pseudonym of Mrs Isobel Christian Johnston, friend of Sir Walter Scott; born in Fife in 1781, and died in 1857.*

8 oz. (2 cups) cornflour (corn-starch)
6 oz. (⅔ cup) butter
4 oz. (½ cup) caster sugar

1 teasp. baking powder
grated rind of 1 small lemon
2 beaten eggs

Beat the butter until creamy, then work in the sugar, and beat well. Add the lemon rind. Mix the baking powder into the cornflour and add it alternately with the beaten eggs to the butter and sugar mixture. (If the eggs are small a tablespoon of milk may be needed, if the mixture is very stiff.) Half fill 24 small greased patty tins, or paper cases. Bake in a hot oven (425° F.) for about 10 minutes.

Makes about 24.

DUNDEE MARMALADE

Dundee is the home of bitter orange marmalade, its invention being credited to Mr and Mrs James Keiller in the early eighteenth century. Story has it that a ship from Spain took refuge from a storm in Dundee harbour, carrying a large cargo of Seville oranges. These were bought in quantity, very cheaply, by James Keiller, who later found that owing to their bitterness he was unable to sell them. His ingenious wife, Janet, not wishing to waste the fruit, made them into a jam, or conserve, little realizing that it would achieve world fame and that her descendants would still be making it today.

2 lb. Seville or bitter oranges	4 pt (8 cups) water
2 lemons	4 lb. preserving sugar

Wash the oranges and lemons and put, whole, into a large saucepan or preserving pan, add the water, and put the lid on. Bring to the boil and simmer for about 1½ hours so that you can easily pierce the fruit. When they are ready, take them out and leave them on a big dish to cool. With a sharp knife, slice them into the thickness yo like,[1] and remove any pips. Add these pips to the juice, boil for minutes, then strain. Add the sliced fruit to the juice and bring to th boil; then add the sugar. Stir over a gentle heat until it is dissolve then boil up rapidly, without stirring, for about ½ hour, or unt setting point (approximately 220° F.) is attained. A small spoonf put on to a cold saucer will 'wrinkle' up when the dish is tilted – the marmalade is cooked enough. Pour into warmed jars, and cov at once. Makes about 4 lb.

Marmalade sauce (see page 18) is excellent with roasted duck, po or ham.

Dundee is also famous for its fruit cake (see page 1).

[1] The fruit for this marmalade should be coarsely cut, which gives the characteristic bitter taste.

ARBROATH SMOKIES

These are quite unlike any other smoked fish in the world. Small haddocks are used, the fish are cleaned, but not split open, salted, then tied in twos by the tails, hung high on little wooden spits or over halved whisky barrels above a fire usually made from oak or silver-birch chips. This method originated at Auchmithie, but by the beginning of the nineteenth century the fisherfolk settled at Arbroath, and by the end of that century the success of these fish became more widely known, and the name was changed to Arbroath smokies. The outside of an Arbroath smokie is a lovely copper colour, and the inside has a most delectable savoury flavour and creamy texture. When the pit or barrels were not available, ingenious fisherwives set up their own small smoking shed as in the photograph.

It is difficult to obtain these delicacies outside Scotland, but if you are fortunate enough to find them, the traditional method of cooking is either to steam them, or heat them in a gentle oven or under a moderate grill, then split open and remove the backbone. Dust with black pepper, add a knob of butter, close up and heat through again. The fish has already been cooked in the long smoking process, so does not want to be made dry by further cooking. *Bon appetit!*

HAM AND HADDIE

An unusual combination which really works. It originates from the Moray Firth.

1 large smoked haddock (the pale Moray Firth kind is best)	2 large slices smoked ham
a little water	2 tablesp. butter
	black pepper

The most convenient way of cooking this so that there are no bones or skin, is first to put the haddock, skin side down, in a large flat pan and barely cover with water, then bring to the boil and simmer for 2 minutes on each side. Remove the fish and take off the skin and all the bones. Then heat the butter in a frying-pan and lay the ham slices in it, turning once: then put the fish on top, season with freshly milled black pepper, cover and simmer gently for about minutes.

Serves 2.

I often pour about $\frac{1}{2}$ cup thick cream on top, and then brown under a hot grill before serving. This makes a delicious sauce with the ham and haddie.

Poached egg is also served with poached Finnan Haddie in Scotland

Outside the smoking shed, Arbroath, c. 1890

On the Caledonian Canal, near Inverness, 189

COLLOPS-IN-THE-PAN

Scotch beef is world famous, Aberdeen Angus and Belted Galloway cattle producing some of the finest beef there is. This recipe is from Meg Dods's The Cook and Housewife's Manual, *1826. Only prime steak should be used to savour this dish at its best.*

8 thin slices of rump or fillet steak (cut about ¼ in. thick)
2 tablesp. butter
4 medium sliced onions
black pepper and salt

1 tablesp. walnut pickle (the juice from pickled walnuts) *or* mushroom ketchup, *or* oyster juice

Melt the butter in a large frying-pan and let it get hot, then add the sliced onions, and when they are softened but not coloured, push them aside and add the steaks. Let them brown quickly on both sides, add pepper, then spread the onions around and amongst them. Cover, and cook gently for about 10 minutes. Take off the lid, put the steaks on to a warmed dish and keep them warm, then add the walnut pickle and salt to taste. Boil up for 1 minute only, then pour over the steaks.

Serves 4.

BLACK BUN

Black Bun is a rich and delicious fruit cake formerly eaten on Twelfth Night, but nowadays served at Hogmanay. It should be made several weeks before it is wanted, like a Christmas cake, so that it can mature. See also: Het Pint and Haggis, page 59.

Recipe from Miss Daisy Welland.

FOR THE CASING

8 oz. (2 cups) flour
4 oz. (½ cup) butter
½ teasp. baking powder

a little cold water
1 beaten egg for finishing

TO MAKE THE CASING

Rub the butter into the flour, add baking powder and mix to a stiff paste with water (about 4 tablespoons). Put on to a floured board, and roll out to a thin sheet. Grease a loaf tin 8 in. square and line with the pastry, keeping back enough for the lid.

FOR THE FILLING

2 lb. seedless raisins
3 lb. currants
½ lb. chopped blanched almonds
¾ lb. (3 cups, scant) flour
½ lb. (1 cup) sugar
2 teasp. Jamaica pepper (allspice)
1 teasp. ground ginger

1 teasp. ground cinnamon
¼ teasp. black pepper
1 flat teasp. cream of tartar
1 flat teasp. baking powder
1 tablesp. brandy
¼ pt. (½ cup) milk

TO PREPARE THE FILLING

Mix all the filling ingredients together except the milk. Then a just enough milk to moisten the mixture. Put it into the lined tin a put the pastry lid on top, damping the edges well to make it sti Prick all over with a fork, and with a thin skewer make four ho right down to the bottom of the cake, brush with beaten egg a cook in a slow (225° F.) oven for about 3 hours. It will keep fo year in an airtight tin.

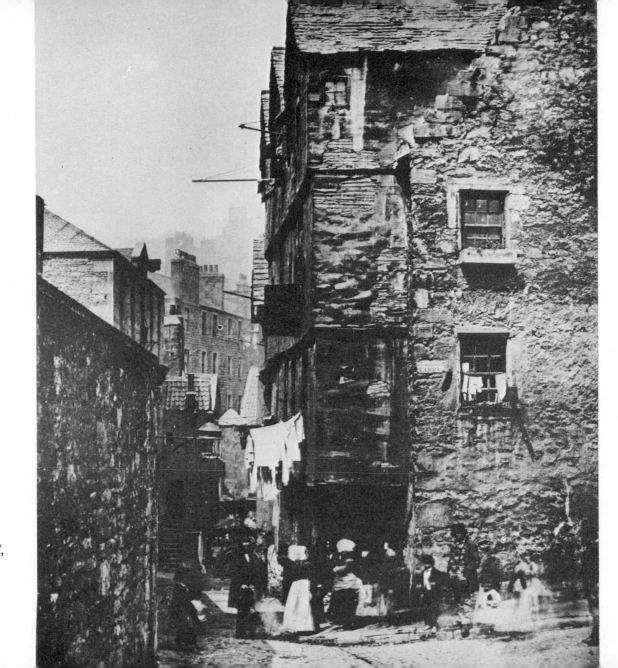

igh School Yards Wynd,
dinburgh, c. 1845

FISH SOUP

Often made with the young of the coalfish, known in Scotland as saithe, which is a first cousin of the cod. When young they have a very marine flavour not unlike a mussel. Any white fish can be used, fresh young haddock being particularly good.

1 small haddock (about 3 lb.), filleted, but the head and bones retained
1 pt. (2 cups) fish stock
1 pt. (2 cups) milk
1 small carrot
1 stalk celery
1 medium onion

1 heaped tablesp. butter
1 tablesp. flour
2 tablesp. chopped parsley
salt and pepper
4 slices of bread fried in butter, then diced, as garnish
4 tablesp. cream (optional)

Simmer the bones and head in 2 pt. (4 cups) water with salt and pepper and the vegetables, all finely diced, for about 1 hour, or until the vegetables are well cooked and mushy, and the liquid reduced by half. Strain, and reserve the stock. Melt the butter, stir in the flour, and gradually add the warm fish stock, stirring all the time until it is smooth, then add the milk, and do likewise. Lightly poach the fillets, for no more than 10 minutes, season to taste, add the parsley, but do not cook it so that it loses colour, and serve hot, allowing one fillet or equivalent per person. Garnish with 1 tablespoon cream for each dish, and serve scattered with the diced, fried croûtons.

Serves 4.

Crofter's house, Loch Ewe, Ross and Cromarty, c. 188

BUTTERSCOTCH

2 lb. brown sugar
½ lb. (1 cup) butter, creamed

juice of 1 lemon or 1 heaped teasp. ground ginger

Dissolve the sugar in a saucepan, and when liquid add the butter and flavouring, keep boiling, gently, stirring all the time for about 20 minutes or until it hardens when a little is dropped into ice-cold water. Then beat very well for about 5 minutes, pour on to a buttered slab or tin, and when cool mark into squares with a knife. When cold and set, remove, and tap the bottom with a heavy knife handle to break up.

Makes about 2 lb. butterscotch.

TABLET OR TAIBLET

A traditional Scots toffee which can be flavoured according to taste with: cinnamon, clove, ginger, lemon, orange, peppermint, vanilla or nuts.

½ lb. (1 cup) butter or margarine
1 pt. (2 cups) water
1 lb. caster (extra fine) sugar

1 lb. tin sweetened condensed milk such as Nestlé's

Put the butter and water into a deep pan and melt on a low heat. When melted add the sugar and bring to the boil, stirring slowly all the time. When boiling, add the condensed milk and simmer for 25 minutes, stirring to prevent sticking. Take off the heat and add flavouring of your choice, then beat very well for 5 minutes. Pour into a greased pan and score as above, or into little bars about 5 in. long and 1½ in. wide. Wrap each bar in waxed paper when cold.

Makes about 4 lb. of toffee.

The boys of Kilmore, Argyllshire, c. 1860

BROONIE

An Orkney traditional oatmeal gingerbread. The word comes from the Norse Bruni, *meaning a thick bannock.*

6 oz. (1½ cups) medium oatmeal
2 heaped tablesp. butter
1 scant teasp. baking powder
1 beaten egg
a pinch of salt
6 oz. (1½ cups) white flour

4 oz. (½ cup) sugar
2 tablesp. black treacle
   (molasses)
½ pt. (1 cup) approx. buttermilk
1 heaped teasp. ground ginger

In a large bowl mix the oatmeal and flour thoroughly, then rub in the butter, and add the sugar, salt, the ginger and the baking powder. Mix very well. Melt the treacle until warm, then stir in the beaten egg, and half the buttermilk. Stir this mixture into the flour, adding more buttermilk gradually, until the mixture is soft enough to drop from a spoon. (You may need slightly more or less buttermilk according to the size of the egg, the quality of the flour etc.) Well grease a tin about 8 in. long by 4 in. wide, put the mixture in and bake in a moderate oven (350° F.) for about 1¼ hours or until it is well risen and cooked in the centre if a thin skewer is put in. Let it cool for a few minutes before removing from the tin when cooked, cool on a rack, and if possible leave overnight before cutting to let it 'set'.

...ling with locally made roller and oxen, Orkneys, c. 1900

Lady Forbes and friends, Newe, c. 19

QUENELLES

Quenelles are another inheritance from Scotland's links with France which go back dynastically to the marriage of William the Lion to a French wife in 1186, and continue for many hundreds of years afterwards. The name is found in both France and Scotland, and is thought to come from the Anglo-Saxon knyll, meaning 'to pound', for all the ingredients for these very light little dumplings are well pounded before cooking.

They can be made from meat, poultry, game, fish, or cheese and potato. This recipe is from Lady Forbes's private papers: the mixture can be made into small, separate quenelles, or one large one as desired.

1 lb. raw minced meat, poultry, game, fish, etc.	½ lb. butter
	2 egg yolks
2 cups fresh breadcrumbs soaked in a little milk and squeezed dry	4 eggs, separated
	a pinch of nutmeg
	salt and pepper

Pound together the meat, butter and breadcrumbs, then add the 2 egg yolks and mix well. Add the other 4 egg yolks, salt, pepper and a little nutmeg to taste and pound and mix again. Finally add the 4 egg whites, stiffly beaten, and fold thoroughly into the mixture. Make into little oval shapes with 2 dessertspoons, and put into a lightly buttered shallow pan. Pour boiling stock or water over, very gently, to cover, lay a piece of buttered paper or foil on top, and poach very gently for 10 minutes. Take out with a perforated spoon, and serve on a bed of buttered, boiled peas, mixed with chopped mushrooms. If 1 large quenelle is wanted, pour the mixture into a basin, cover, and steam gently for about 40 minutes. Serve with mushroom sauce (see page 77). They can also be served cold after poaching. Put them when drained into the dish they will be served from, and when cool, pour over 1 pt. of jellied stock, or 2 tablespoons aspic powder dissolved in 1 pt. boiling water. Leave in a cold place to set.

Serves 4.

LORRAINE SOUP

Lorraine soup (see end-papers) is also a French inheritance: the name possibly derives from Mary of Lorraine (1515–60), wife of James V of Scotland and mother of Mary Stuart, although some early manuscripts spell it à la Reine, it is thought after Marguerite de Valois. 'I have just now lying on the Table before me, a Receipt for making Soupe à la Reine, copy'd with my own Hand.' David Hume, philosopher and gastronome, Edinburgh, 1769.

HET PINT

... it was uncanny and would certainly have felt it very uncomfortable, [n]ot to welcome the New Year in the midst of his family, and a few old [f]riends, with the immemorial libation of a het pint.'

Sir Walter Scott.

[T]he het pint was carried through the streets at Hogmanay, in large [c]opper kettles, known as toddy kettles, several hours before midnight.

[ ] pt. mild ale	3 eggs
[ ] teasp. grated nutmeg	½ pt. whisky
[ ] oz. (½ cup) sugar	

[P]ut the ale into a thick saucepan, then add the nutmeg, and bring to [j]ust below boiling-point. (If it boils, the alcoholic content is con[s]iderably lowered.) Stir in the sugar and let it dissolve. Beat the eggs [v]ery well, and add them gradually to the beer, stirring all the time [s]o that it doesn't curdle. Then add the whisky, and heat up, but on [n]o account boil. Pour the liquid from the saucepan into heated [t]ankards, back and forth so that it becomes clear and sparkling. It [c]an also be made using white wine instead of ale and substituting [b]randy for whisky.

HAGGIS

[T]his is perhaps the most traditional of all foods eaten in Scotland at [H]ogmanay (New Year's Eve). It is really a large, round sausage, the skin being the paunch of a sheep. The name Hogmanay is thought by some to have come from the Old French aguil' anneuf through Norman-French hoguigané – 'to the New Year'. Haggis probably derives from the French hachis, 'to chop'.

The finest haggis of all is made with deer's liver instead of sheep's liver. It is always served to the swirl of a kilted Highlander playing the bagpipes, and it is customary to drink small glasses of neat whisky between mouthfuls.

Lady Login's receipt, 1856

1 cleaned sheep or lamb's stomach bag	the heart and lights of the sheep boiled and minced
2 lb. dry oatmeal	1 large chopped onion
1 lb. chopped mutton suet	½ teasp. each: cayenne pepper,
1 lb. lamb's or deer's liver, boiled and minced	Jamaica pepper, salt and pepper
1 pt. (2 cups) stock	

Toast the oatmeal slowly until it is crisp, then mix all ingredients (except the stomach bag) together, and add the stock. Fill the bag to just over half full, press out the air and sew up securely. Have ready a large pot full of boiling water, prick the haggis all over with a large needle, so that it does not burst, and boil slowly for 4 to 5 hours. It is often served with Clapshot (see page 88).

Serves about 12 (see also Black Bun, page 48).

[J]ames Ballantyne, poet, Dr G. Bell and David Octavius Hill, photographer, c. 1845. Photograph by D. O. Hill. James Ballantyne and [h]is brother John were well known in Edinburgh in Sir Walter Scott's time, for their hospitality and lavish dinner parties.

Herrings

'It's nae fish ye're buying, it's men's lives.'
The Antiquary, *Sir Walter Scott.*

Herrings are almost the national fish of Scotland and treated in any number of ways. When salted and smoked they are called 'Red' herrings, and were for many centuries the staple diet of poor people, for the very strong taste kept away hunger. They were soaked overnight, then boiled on top of potatoes in their jackets, (known as 'Tatties an' Herrin''), or eaten with jacket-baked potatoes, the bland vegetable taking away much of the saltiness. As the public taste for less salty fish became evident, the herring was only lightly salted and smoked for about 8 hours. Whe cured closed up they are called Bloaters, but when split open befor curing they are Kippers. The finest kippers are pale in colour and con from Lochfyneside. They can be grilled, fried or lightly cooked in boilin water, and are excellent served with scrambled eggs. Kippers entire soaked in fresh lemon juice overnight, can be drained, sliced and eate like smoked salmon on bread and butter. They require no other prepara tion, except to remove the backbone. Fresh herrings can be stuffed an baked, grilled, or fried after rolling in oatmeal like trout (see page 12 when fried or grilled they are served with mustard sauce (page 88).

PICKLED OR POTTED HERRINGS

8 fresh herrings
2 bay leaves
$\frac{1}{4}$ pt. ($\frac{1}{2}$ cup) water
$\frac{1}{2}$ pt. (1 cup) white vinegar

1 teasp. peppercorns
$\frac{1}{2}$ teasp. pickling spice
1 medium onion
salt and pepper

Clean and fillet the herrings, sprinkle the flesh with a little salt and pepper, then roll them up from tail to head and put on top of the bay leaves in a fireproof dish. Pack them tightly so they do not unrol sprinkle the peppercorns and spices among them, also the finel sliced onion. Pour over the vinegar and water mixed, cover with fo or a lid, and bake in a moderate oven (325° F.) for 30–40 minute Leave to get cold in the liquid and serve with a little poured ove each fish. Mackerel can also be treated in the same way.

Serves 4.

...erwives, Ullapool, c. 1890

Carlyle and friends on the steps of St Brycedale House, 1

HOWTOWDIE

A method of cooking chicken which has a decidedly French influence. The name is thought to come from the Old French hutaudeau, *a pullet. In the nineteenth century it was dished with poached eggs, and called Howtowdie wi' Drappit eggs'. The bird can be stuffed if liked before cooking.*

1 roasting chicken about 4 lb.
6 button onions or shallots
4 oz. (½ cup) butter
2 whole cloves
6 black peppercorns
pinch of mace
1 pt. (2 cups) boiling giblet stock
chicken's liver
2 tablesp. thick cream (optional)
2 lb. spinach
salt and pepper

FOR THE STUFFING
2 oz. (2 cups) fresh breadcrumbs
1 small chopped shallot
1 teasp. chopped tarragon
1 teasp. chopped parsley
a little milk
salt and pepper

For the stuffing, soak the breadcrumbs in just enough milk to moisten them and make them swell. Then add all the other stuffing ingredients and put this into the bird. Secure with a small skewer. Put the butter, all but 1 level tablespoon, in a casserole, let it melt and add the onions. Let them gently brown then put the chicken in the middle. Roast in a hot (400° F.) oven for 20 minutes, turning frequently until lightly browned, then add the mace, cloves, seasonings and stock. Cover and cook in a moderate (350° F.) oven for about 40 minutes or until done. Meanwhile, cook the spinach, drain it well and keep hot. Remove the bird from the oven and strain off stock into a saucepan. Add the liver, chopped, to the stock and cook it gently for 5 minutes, then mash it so that it absorbs the stock; add the cream and remaining butter cut into small pieces, reheat, but do not boil.

Dress the drained and seasoned spinach around the edges of an oval dish, put the chicken in the middle and pour the sauce over the bird but not over the spinach. If you wish to try the 'Drappit eggs' poach them in the stock, *before* adding the liver, and keep them warm on the spinach before serving.

Serves 6.

' "Not a dish for every day," someone may remark. Assuredly not. The longer one lives, the more one realises that nothing is a dish for every day.'
Birds and Beasts of the Greek Anthology
Norman Douglas, 1868–1952.

Playing marbles outside Cumberland House, Aberdeen, 1857, named after the Duke of Cumberland. He and his officers used the whole house as lodgings on his way to Culloden. It is now a museum. Cumberland House was leased by the town in 1836 as a home for destitute boys. This was achieved by a gift of 1,000 guineas from Dr G. Watt, of Old Deer, Aberdeenshire

PORRIDGE

'. . . Chief o' Scotia's food', as Robbie Burns described it, is eaten all over Scotland, and indeed in many other parts of the world. It was no doubt the mainstay of the little destitute boys in the photograph on the opposite page.

There are many traditions to porridge-making and porridge-eating; for instance, it must always be stirred when cooking with the right hand, clockwise. The stirring is done with a straight wooden stick, like a wooden spoon with the spoon cut off, known in various parts of Scotland as a spurtle or a theevil. Porridge is always spoken of as 'they', and an old custom demands that 'they' are eaten standing up. It is usually made with oatmeal, but in Caithness, Orkney and Shetland bere-meal (a kind of barley) is often used. Porridge has various names in different parts of the country: Gaelic *brochan* in the Highlands; milgruel (Shetland) and tartan-purry is thin porridge made with the liquor in which kail has been cooked. Traditionally porridge was eaten from a birch-wood bowl with a horn spoon. It is served with *cold* milk or cream, sugar or, more often, salt; and as with all foods, the fresher and better the oatmeal, the better the porridge. Many Scotsmen like a glass of porter, stout or beer with it.

FOR ONE PERSON (large country portion)

1¼ oz. (¼ cup) medium oatmeal   1 cup water
a pinch of salt

Boil the water in a saucepan, and when it is bubbling add the oatmeal in a constant stream with the left hand stirring all the time with the right. When it is all boiling regularly, pull to the side of the heat, cover and simmer very gently for 10 minutes, then add the salt and stir. Cover again, and simmer very gently for about another 10 minutes; the time cannot be more precise as the quality of the oats varies in cooking time. Serve piping hot in cold soup plates, and dip each spoonful into individual bowls of cold milk or cream before eating. This is the method which has been used for centuries. Porridge can also be made in a double boiler, which prevents any fear of burning.

Porridge served in Scotland is much thinner than in Ireland or England, and I think better that way. Also the large flake oatmeal used in other countries is nothing like so good as the medium-size variety in Scotland.

EDINBURGH ROCK

Traditionally made since the eighteenth century by the Edinburgh firm of Ferguson.

1 lb. (2 cups) of either granulated or crushed lump sugar	1½ gills (¾ cup) water ½ teasp. cream of tartar

FLAVOURS AND COLOURS TO TASTE

a pinch or a few drops of each:

ginger	– fawn	peppermint	– green
raspberry	– pink	lemon	– pale yellow
orange	– orange or yellow	vanilla	– white

Heat the sugar and water until the sugar is dissolved. When just about to boil add the cream of tartar and boil without stirring until it reaches 250° F., or until it forms a hard ball in cold water. Take from the heat and add whatever colouring you wish, remembering that the colour will fade as the candy is 'pulled'. Pour on to a buttered marble slab, or into buttered candy bars (obtainable at shops selling confectionary equipment). Cool slightly and turn the edges to the centre with an oiled scraper, but do not stir. When cool enough to handle, dust it with icing (confectioner's) sugar, and 'pull' it evenly and quickly, taking care not to twist it, until it becomes opaque and dull. This should be done in a warm kitchen, or near a heater if the candy becomes stiff too quickly. Draw out the candy into strips and cut into 1- or 2-in. lengths with a pair of oiled scissors. Leave in warm room on greased paper for at least 24 hours, when the rock will become powdery and soft. It can be stored in an air-tight tin. If the candy remains sticky, it means that it has not been pulled enough. It is not really difficult to make, once you have acquired the habit, and it is an ideal occupation for children on a wet afternoon, especially if each child is allowed to pick his or her own colour.

Day by the Sea at West Pans, April 1885. Photograph by Mr Aird

SOLAN GOOSE

St Kilda, from the Gaelic Hirta, the western land, is a small island off the Outer Hebrides, now no longer inhabited. On 29th August 1930 the few Gaelic-speaking inhabitants were resettled, at their own request, mainly in Morvern parish, Argyllshire. The island has been in the possession of the Macleods, except for the period 1779 to 1871.

What the reindeer is to the Lapps, so the gannet or solan goose was to the St Kildan. These large sea-birds were preserved for all-the-year consumption by being slightly salted, then wind-blown (blawn). They were put into beehive-shaped earth cells, known as cleits, which allowed for adequate circulation of air. Some six hundred of these cleits are still standing. As well as eating the birds both fresh and dried, the islanders ate the eggs in quantity. In 1697, 16,000 eggs and 22,600 birds were eaten annually. The feathers were used for pillows and eiderdowns.

The traveller Sands took three apples to St Kilda in 1875, the first to be seen there. Until the middle of the nineteenth century they knew not what a pig, or a bee, or a rabbit, or a rat, looked like.

The solan goose (Morus bassana) breeds on many rocky islands around our coast, also on the Faroe Islands and in the Gulf of St Lawrence. In 1618 John Taylor, the 'Waterman' poet, described them as: 'Most delicate fowls which has very good flesh. . . .' Sir William Jardine in 1845, wrote: 'We have eaten them boiled like ham and considered them by no means either strong, fishy or unpalatable.' As late as 1856 the eggs were sold in London, and reputed to have been often eaten at Buckingham Palace. They are still eaten, and the birds still caught in large numbers, for food, on some islands in the Outer Hebrides.

Dulse, sloke and sea-tangle also formed part of the St Kildan's diet (see page 2).

Gannet or solan goose can be cooked in any way as for wild goose or goose. The eggs, which are pale blue in colour, can be served as gulls' eggs: hard-boiled, then shelled when cold, and eaten with salt or celery salt.

Kilda's Parliament, c. 1880

HONEY CAKES

From Lady Clark of Tillypronie, c. 1872. Heather honey is famous for its flavour, and is also used in the making of the liqueur, Drambuie, and Atholl Brose (see page 96).

	FOR THE TOPPING
1 lb. (4 cups) sifted flour	½ lb. (1 cup) thick heather honey
¼ lb. (½ cup) butter	3 tablesp. ground almonds
2 heaped tablesp. caster sugar	*or*
2 tablesp. honey	1 cup melted heather honey
2 egg yolks	
1½ teasp. baking powder	
½ pt. (1 cup) milk	
a pinch of salt	
1 egg white	

Rub the butter into the flour, and gently heat the sugar and honey until it is well mixed, then stir in the baking powder. Add this to the flour mixture, alternately with the egg yolks beaten with the milk. Mix very well, and finally add the salt and mix again. Roll out on a floured board very lightly and cut into rounds or shapes, put on to a greased baking sheet and bake in a moderate oven (350° F.) for about 20 minutes. Remove to a rack, paint the tops with lightly beaten egg white, and spread over the thick honey mixed with the ground almonds. Put in a very cool oven for no longer than 5 minutes to set. Eat either hot or cold.

An alternative method is to serve these light little cakes hot from the oven with warm, melted heather honey poured over.

Makes approximately 24 cakes.

Fair Day at Benbecula, c. 1890

MUTTON PIES

'Fine mutton pies, fat piping hot –
One for a penny, four for a groat!'

[M]utton pies are eaten all over Scotland, and were known in Glasgow in [th]e old days as 'Tuppenny struggles'. They are made with hot-water, or [ra]ised, crust, which can be troublesome to make in cold weather, but [th]e same filling can be used for a pasty or turnover, with short-crust, [or] flaky pastry.

[TO] MAKE THE HOT-WATER PASTRY

[1] lb. plain flour	½ pt. (1 cup) water
[¼] lb. (½ cup) beef dripping or lard	½ teasp. salt

[FI]LLING

[1] lb. lean lamb free from fat, bone, gristle, etc. cut into very small pieces or minced	1 small minced onion or shallot
[Sal]t and freshly ground pepper	½ teasp. ground mace or nutmeg
[1] teasp. Worcestershire sauce or mushroom ketchup	4 tablesp. stock

[T]o make the pastry, put the fat and water into a saucepan and bring [to] the boil. Put the flour and salt into a basin and make a hole in the [m]iddle, pour the boiling water and fat into this, and mix with a [sp]atula until cool enough to handle, then form into a ball. This must [b]e done quickly before the fat hardens too much. Turn on to a floured board, and knead well, then pat into a flat shape. Divide into half and put one half to keep warm. Roll the half out into a large oval, and stand a small jar (about 3 in. across) in the middle. Mould the pastry up the sides to a height of about 3 in. and when it stands well remove the jar, and make another mould in the same way. Roll out the lids, cutting them into rounds to fit the top. Mix all the filling ingredients together and fill the pastry moulds. Damp the edges and pinch the top on. Make a slit in the centre to let the steam out and brush the top with milk or beaten egg to colour it. Bake on a baking sheet in a slow oven (250° F.) so that the inside has time to cook, about 45 minutes. Whilst cooking roll out the remainder of the pastry and proceed in the same way.

Makes about 4 pies.

If using short crust pastry, use 1 lb. flour and ½ lb. shortening or fat, a pinch of salt, and about ½ cup cold water to make a firm paste. Roll out on to a floured board, and cut into circles about 6 in. in diameter. Fill half the circles with the filling, damp the edges and fold over, crimping with a fork to secure them. Brush with egg, and bake as above.

FORFAR BRIDIES

These are made with finely chopped beef instead of lamb and are made with short-crust pastry, like a turnover. The amounts given above make about 8 bridies. Cooked or raw venison can also be used for these pasties.

'Showing the flag' at Newe, Strathdon, Aberdeenshire, 19

CHOCOLATE CAKE

Recipe of Rosa Mattravers, cook to Lady Forbes of Newe from 1900 to 1921.

½ lb. (1 cup) butter
½ lb. (1 cup) caster sugar
7 eggs, separated
½ lb. grated chocolate Meunier
  (bitter chocolate)

½ lb. blanched, slightly browned,
  chopped almonds
4 oz. (1 cup, generous) sifted
  flour
a pinch of salt

Beat the butter to a cream and work in the sugar. Then add the beaten egg yolks, beating well all the time. Add the grated chocolate, the chopped almonds, and salt. Now whip the egg whites very stiff and add lightly, and alternately with the flour. Pour into a well-greased cake tin (lined with greaseproof paper), and bake in a moderate (325° F.) oven for about 1½ hours.

Newhaven fisherwives, c. 1845. Photograph by D. O. Hi

NEWHAVEN CREAM

lb. steamed, boned smoked
haddock[1]
oz. (1 cup) breadcrumbs
oz. (½ cup) butter
pt. (1½ cups) milk or light
cream
eggs
t and pepper

FOR THE SAUCE[1]
1 heaped tablesp. butter
2 tablesp. flour
1 pt. (2 cups) warm milk
2 tablesp. chopped parsley
salt and pepper

ake up the fish, and mash it lightly, then add the breadcrumbs.
ason to taste. Melt the butter in the milk and pour over, mixing
ll. Then add the well-beaten eggs. Pour into either 1 large
ttered basin, or several small ones, put foil over the top, and steam
er boiling water for 1 hour if large, and ½ hour if small. Remove
e foil, and put a warm plate on the top, then tip over, to unmould.
rve hot with the sauce of your choice.

Serves 4.

TO MAKE THE SAUCE

Melt the butter and stir in the flour, let it cook for 1 minute, then
pour in gradually the warm milk, stirring all the time until it is
smooth and thick. Season to taste, and finally add the parsley. Pour
over the creams and serve at once. Mushroom sauce can also be
served. It is made as parsley sauce using 4 oz. chopped mushrooms
instead of parsley, and simmering gently until they are cooked.

The small creams make an excellent first course if served cold, and
set into aspic. They should be unmoulded as above, and when cold
masked with 1 tablespoon aspic powder dissolved in ½ pt. boiling
water, left until it is the consistency of a raw egg white before
pouring over. Chill, until jellied.

[1] Salmon can also be used instead of haddock, and egg sauce (*see*
page 101) is sometimes served instead of the parsley.

SELKIRK BANNOCK

Selkirk Bannock is quite unlike the oatcake bannock (see page 102) for it is a yeasted fruit loaf, round and flat, first made by Robbie Douglas in his bakery in Selkirk Market Place in 1859. A slice of Selkirk Bannock was all that Queen Victoria would eat when she visited Sir Walter Scott's granddaughter at Abbotsford, in 1867, and was offered an elegant repast.

It was originally made only with the finest sultanas imported from Turkey. Nowadays a little candied orange peel is also sometimes added.

2 lb. flour
1 oz. yeast
½ teasp. sugar for creaming the yeast
4 oz. (½ cup) butter
4 oz. (½ cup) lard

½ pt. warmed (tepid) milk
½ lb. (1 cup) sugar
1 lb. sultanas or seedless raisins
4 oz. (1 cup) chopped candied orange peel (optional)
a little milk and sugar for glazing

Melt the butter and lard until soft but not oily, then add the milk warmed to blood heat; cream the yeast with the ½ teaspoon sugar and add to the milk and butter mixture. Sift the flour into a bowl, make a well in the centre and pour in the liquid, then sprinkle the flour from the sides over the top to make a batter. Cover with a cloth and leave in a warm place for about 1 hour, or until it has doubled in size. Knead well, and add the fruit and the remaining sugar (both slightly warmed). Knead again for about 5 minutes, then shape into a round flattish shape (if baking in a tin, put into a buttered tin, that it comes to about half-way up), cover and set again in a warm place for about ¾ hour. Bake in a moderate oven (350° F.) for about 1–1½ hours, and half an hour before it is done take it from the oven and brush the top over with a little warm milk which has had a tablespoon sugar dissolved in it. Put back in the oven and continue cooking until it is golden. Test with a skewer in the middle before removing from the heat; the bottom will sound hollow if tapped when it is properly cooked.

Makes 1 loaf about 9 in. across.

STOVED POTATOES

Or Stovies, from the French étouffée, *to stew in a closed vessel.*

The potatoes must be unblemished and of the same size to make this dish successfully.

Peel the potatoes and put them in a saucepan with not more than ½-in. of water. Sprinkle with salt (or use sea-water if available, it gives a unique flavour to potatoes) and dot, quite lavishly, with butter. Cover tightly, and simmer very gently over a low heat until the potatoes are cooked. This time will vary with the type of potato, so the floury variety are the best to use. Shake from time to time to prevent sticking, and examine them after about ½ hour.

In country districts, bacon or meat dripping is first melted, then about 2 medium sliced onions are fried in it until golden but not brown, the potatoes, cut into thick slices, are added with water, salt, as above, the butter being omitted. This is served with cold meats, or as a supper dish on its own. New potatoes are excellent done this way: when ready, shake a handful of fine oatmeal over them, replace lid, then shake well before leaving on the side of the stove for 10 minutes. Serve hot, with ice-cold glasses of buttermilk.

SKIRLIE

Served as an accompaniment to meats, game birds, boiled cod with mustard sauce (*see* page 88), or with creamy, mashed potatoes. The same mixture, uncooked, makes an unusual and delicious stuffing for chicken or boiling mutton. It is very tasty, with a nutty texture. In some parts of Scotland it is called mealie pudding, and it is steamed in a greased basin for 1 hour, before turning out. Individual mealie puddings enclosed in a skin can be bought at shops throughout Scotland.

Put the grated suet or dripping in a very hot pan, and when melted add the onions, and lightly brown them. Then stir in the oatmeal, so that it makes a fairly thick mixture. Keep stirring over a gentle heat for about 5 to 7 minutes until it is all thoroughly cooked and season to taste.

Serves 4 to 6.

8 oz. (2 cups) medium oatmeal
2 finely chopped medium onions
salt

4 oz. grated suet, or 4 tablesp. good dripping
freshly ground pepper

Small spoonfuls can be rolled into a ball and cooked in boiling soup like a dumpling. These dumplings are often served with Scots Broth (*see* page 36).

Planting potatoes, Skye, 1887. Photograph by George Washington Wilson

GALANTINE OF VENISON AND PORK

Mrs Jamieson, 1885.

> '*But old Sir Thomas thought daintier cheer*
> *A pasty made of the good red deer.*'
>
> The Witches Frolic,
> *Reverend R. H. Barham, 1788–1845.*

This recipe can also be used for chopped hare with pork belly; or flank of beef.

3 lb. thick breast venison	1 lb. pork sausage-meat or
½ lb. raw ham or Ayrshire bacon	minced pork
3 hard-boiled eggs	6 black peppercorns
3 cloves garlic	salt and pepper
sprig of thyme and marjoram	2 qt. (8 cups) water

Bone the venison and cut away any gristle. Cube the ham and mix it with the sausage-meat, or minced pork, and garlic. Boil up the venison bones with the water, salt and herbs. Place the boned venison on a board and spread over half the sausage-meat, then the eggs cut in half, then the remainder of the sausage-meat, and season well. Roll up carefully and put in a large floured cloth, tying the ends securely. Place in the venison bone stock, cover, and simmer gently for 4 hours. Leave it to cool in the water. When cold remove from the stock, take off the cloth and place the galantine into a dish which just fits it. Cover with foil and put a weight on top, then chill overnight. Serve cold, cut into slices.

Serves about 8.

Deerstalking at Inverewe, 1890

TEA PANCAKES

...a pancakes are also called 'Scots Crumpets'. They can be made either ...a fairly hot girdle, or in a lightly greased, heavy pan, such as an ...elette pan.

...croft in the Orkneys as described by Captain (later Sir Martin) ...obisher (1535–94) in 1577:

..."Their houses are very simply builded of Pibble Stone, without any ...chimneys, the fire being made in the midst thereof. The good man, ...wife and children, and other of the family, eate and sleeps on the one side of the house, and the cattell on the other. They are destitute of wood, their fire is turffes, and cowshards. They have corn, bigge [Hordeum hexastichon] and otes, with which they pay rent [to the King of the island]. They take great quantitye of fish, which they dry in the wind and sunne. They dresse their meat without salt. . . . They have egges . . . and fowle . . . their bread is eaten in cakes, their drink is ewe's milk, and in some parts ale. . . .'

Pibble stones are large rocks rounded by the sea, which were split by burning.

...b. (2 cups) flour	2 tablesp. melted butter
...ablesp. caster sugar	1 level teasp. salt
...eggs	$\frac{3}{4}$ pt. (1$\frac{1}{2}$ cups) approx. milk, or
...ittle oil or suet to grease	preferably buttermilk
...the girdle or pan	

...rst beat the eggs well, then in another bowl mix the flour, sugar ...d salt, and add slowly and alternately with the melted butter to the ...gs, beating all the time. Pour, in a slow trickle, enough milk or ...ttermilk to make a batter the consistency of thin cream. Mean-...ile, heat up the girdle or set the pan on a hot stove and rub the ...ttom with a piece of suet or pour in not more than a teaspoon of oil for the first four pancakes, repeating this as the batter is used. Beat the batter well, before using and then drop in a large tablespoonful at a time, rolling the pan round so that it is as thin as possible and evenly spread. When golden brown underneath, turn with a spatula and cook the other side. Set them on a clean tea towel or kitchen paper to drain, and cover them. When cool spread with butter, and jam, jelly or honey, and roll up. They should be served fairly soon after making, and should be warm, but not hot.

Makes about 20 pancakes.

Another method uses the eggs separated: the whites beaten until stiff, and added last. This makes a very light, crisp little pancake which melts in the mouth.

BEETROOT SALAD

Lord Elphinstone, 1880.

2 large cooked beetroots

FOR THE SAUCE

2 egg yolks	2 teasp. tarragon vinegar
½ teasp. made English mustard	¼ pt. (½ cup) stiffly whipped
¼ pt. (½ cup) olive oil	cream
2 teasp. chili vinegar	salt and pepper

Do not prick the beetroots in peeling them, or the juice will run out, which spoils the colour. Slice them into the dish they will be served from.

TO MAKE THE SAUCE

Put the egg yolks into a basin and beat well with a whisk: add the mustard, salt and pepper, then drop by drop, add the olive oil, alternately with the two vinegars, beating well with a whisk as for a mayonnaise. It should 'make' in the same way (if it doesn't take, then break another egg yolk and add the mixture, drop by drop, beating all the time). Lastly add the cream, which should be a ¼ pt. *before* whipping. Make the sauce ½ hour before it is wanted and keep cold.

Pour it over the beetroots, but do not mix it through. A pinch sugar can be added to the cream if liked.

Serves 4.

Lord Elphinstone remarks: 'A spendthrift for oil, a miser vinegar, and a lunatic to mix it!' Nowadays an electric mixer co take the place of the lunatic.

Served with cold beef or mutton, or with a savoury such Scotch Woodcock, beetroot salad makes a light meal.

SCOTCH WOODCOCK

8 anchovy fillets	1 tablesp. chopped parsley
4 egg yolks	pinch cayenne pepper
½ pt. (1 cup) thin cream	4 slices toast
1 tablesp. butter	

Pound the anchovy fillets into the butter and add pepper to tas Then spread the toast thinly with this and put on to a warmed pl and keep warm. Beat the egg yolks, cream, parsley and cayen pepper to taste together, and stir over boiling water in a doul boiler until thick. Pour over the toasts and serve at once.

Serves 4.

Lord and Lady Elphinstone with their children at Carberry Tower, 18

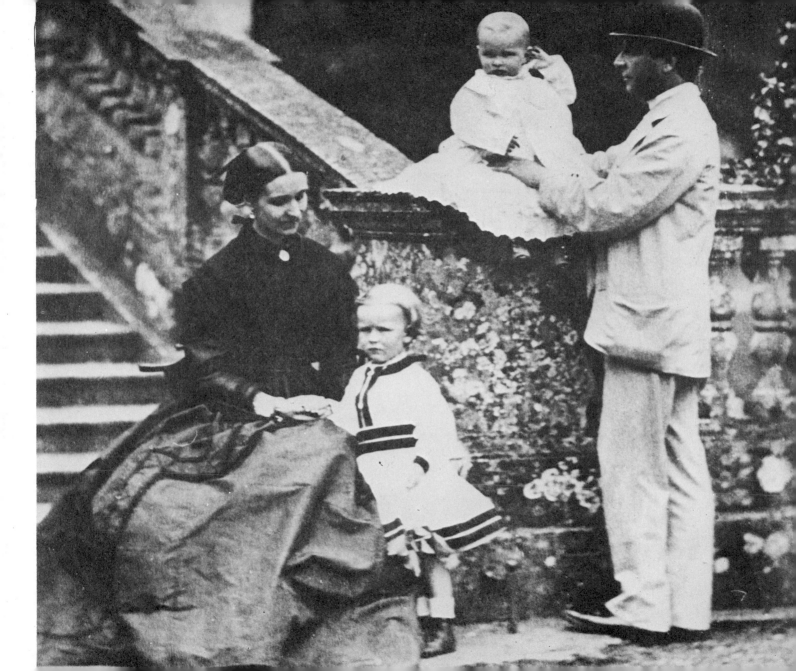

COD WITH MUSTARD SAUCE

Many Norse words have survived in Orkney dialect, and several traditional methods of cooking have a decidedly Norse influence, such as the serving of mustard sauce with boiled or poached cod.

Mrs. Elizabeth Cleland in her book A New and Easy Method of Cookery, *Edinburgh 1759, gives a recipe for poached Scate [sic], 'strewn with parsley, and served with melted butter and mustard, together with anchovy mixed with melted butter, both served in separate jugs.'*

3 lb. fresh cod
½ pt. (1 cup) milk
½ pt. (1 cup) water
a pinch of salt
freshly ground pepper
4 sprigs parsley (left on the stalks)

2 tablesp. butter
1½ tablesp. flour
1 heaped teasp. made English mustard (or more according to taste)

Put the fish in a pan on top of the parsley, for this stops it sticking, add the milk and water mixed, also a little salt, cover, and simmer gently, turning once so that the fish is cooked evenly, for about 10 minutes depending on the thickness of the cut. Remove the fish to a warmed dish and keep warm. (If wanted off the bone and skinned, now is the time to do it, then keep it warm in a low oven with a piece of foil on top.) Melt the butter, stir in the flour and the mustard, then add the warm fish liquor, stir all the time until it thickens and is creamy. Add pepper to taste. Either put the fish back in the sauce to heat up, or pour the sauce over. This is often served with Skirlie (*see* page 80) and Clapshot, another traditional Orkney dish.

Serves 4 to 6.

CLAPSHOT

1 lb. potatoes
1 tablesp. chopped chives *or* 4 shallots (chpd and cooked)
1 lb. white turnips

1 heaped tablesp. butter or dripping
salt and pepper to taste

Cook the vegetables separately, drain and then mash them very well together, adding all the other ingredients. Season to taste, and serve very hot.

Serves 4 to 6.

tromness Harbour, Orkney Islands, in the days of sail, 1900

The Misses Binney and Miss Munro, c. 1845. Photograph by D. O. Hil

CALEDONIAN CREAM

1 lb. (2 cups generous) curds or cottage cheese

2 tablesp. generous, Dundee marmalade (*see* page 42)

2 tablesp. sugar

2 tablesp. brandy or Highland unblended malt whisky

1 tablesp. lemon juice

Mix all ingredients together well, and beat with a whisk. Put into a dish and freeze.

Serves 4 to 6.

BAPS

Glasgow is reputed to be the home of the tea-room, the coffee-houses of the eighteenth and nineteenth centuries being used only by men. Miss Cranston, later Mrs Cochrane, is said to have been the pioneer, and in 1884 she rented rooms in Aitkin's Hotel, Argyle Street, for her tea-shop which was so successful that she later acquired not only the whole building, but also other premises in Buchanan Street, Ingram Street and Sauchiehall Street. Yet another Glasgow citizen was a pioneer in eating-houses, for about 1850 William Lang opened the first sandwich and snack bar, referred to by the writer William Makepeace Thackeray as '. . . fifty separate ways of spoiling one's dinner'.

Baps are yeasted rolls, eaten all over Scotland.

1 lb. (4 cups) sifted flour	1 teasp. salt
2 heaped tablesp. lard	1 teasp. sugar
1 oz. yeast or 1 package	½ pt. tepid milk

Mix the flour and salt in a warm bowl, and cream the sugar and yeast together. Heat the lard and when melted add rather less than half the tepid milk to it. Make a well in the middle of the flour and put in the yeast, milk and lard, and mix well with a wooden spoon or the hands. Knead until smooth, scatter a sprinkling of flour over, cover, and set in a warm place to rise for 1 hour. Turn out on to a floured board, knead lightly, then form into oval shapes about 3 in. long and 2 in. wide. Put on to a baking sheet, brush with milk, and if liked floury, dust them with a sprinkling of flour. Leave again for 15 minutes, make a small dent in the middle with your finger, an bake in a hot (400° F.) oven for 15 to 20 minutes.

Makes about 10 baps.

ADELAIDE SANDWICHES

Recipe from Lady Clark 1876. Anchovies can be used instead chicken.

1 cup left-over cooked, diced chicken and ham *or* tongue and chicken	FOR THE SAUCE
	1 tablesp. flour
2 heaped tablesp. butter	1 heaped tablesp. butter
1 heaped tablesp. grated Parmesan cheese	1 teasp. curry paste
4 slices crustless bread	½ pt. (1 cup) warm milk
4 tablesp. cooking oil	

Melt the butter for the sauce, stir in the flour, then add the warr milk stirring all the time. Season to taste; add the curry paste, an the chopped chicken and ham. Then melt 1 tablesp. butter and th oil and fry the bread on one side only. Put the chicken mixtu between the two slices, the fried side uppermost. Then rub th remaining butter with the cheese and spread over the two sand wiches, and brown under the grill.

Serves 2.

Jamaica Bridge, Glasgow, 189

HOTCH-POTCH

Also called Hairst Bree, meaning harvest broth.
> *'A truly delicious soup, quite peculiar to Scotland . . .'*
> *J. G. Lockhart, 1819.*

The essence of this soup-stew is that it must be made with good, fresh meat, and at the time when all the vegetables are very young and crisp. In some parts of Scotland small cabbage is used instead of cauliflower, and in both Harris and Lewis young nettle tops, wild spinach, shemis (Ligusticum scoticum), a kind of wild lovage, wild carrot and garlic have also been used when fresh green vegetables were scarce.

2 lb. neck of lamb chops	1 medium cauliflower
2 cups fresh shelled green peas	4 small yellow turnips
1 cup shelled young broad beans	4 medium carrots
1 small hearty lettuce	6 spring onions (with green)
2 teasp. chopped mint	1 tablesp. chopped parsley
1 teasp. salt and ½ teasp. pepper	1 teasp. sugar
2½ qt. (10 cups) water	

Boil the lamb with the salt and water, very gently, and remove an scum from the top. Cover, and simmer for 1 hour. (If liked, th meat can then be removed and taken from the bone before replacing but this is not traditional.) Add the chopped turnips, carrots, onions beans and half the peas, cover again and simmer for 1½ hours. The add the cauliflower cut into flowerlets, the shredded lettuce, the res of the peas, sugar, mint and season again to taste. Cover, and simme gently for about ½ hour, or until the vegetables and meat are tender but not broken up. Add the parsley just before serving to give a nic fresh taste. The soup-stew should be very thick, and is a meal on it own.

Serves 4 to 6.

On the island of Lewis in the nineteenth-century tea drinking wa thought to be sinful and was only done in secret. The day started with dram (of whisky) known as a 'skalch' in the Highlands.

The beginning of a length of Harris Tweed, c. 188.

WHISKY PUNCH (cold)

Peel 3 lemons finely and squeeze out the juice, then put them in a large jug with ½ lb. sugar. Pour 2 pt. boiling water over, and leave until cold. Strain into a large bowl and add a bottle of Scotch whisky, stirring well. Chill for at least 1 hour.

ATHOLL BROSE

Famous since 1475, named after the then Duke of Atholl who captured his great enemy, the Earl of Ross, by filling the well at which Ross was known to drink with this potent libation. Ross drank deeply of this magical liquor and was taken. This recipe was given by the 8th Duke of Atholl.

3 oz. (3 heaped tablesp.) oatmeal	whisky to make up 1 qt.
2 tablesp. liquid heather honey	1 pt. water (approx.)

Put the oatmeal into a bowl and mix with the water until it is a thick paste. Let it stand for about ½ hour then put it through a fine strainer pressing down well with a spoon so that the oatmeal is quite dry. Throw away the meal, and mix the liquid with the run honey, and stir with a *silver* spoon until well blended. Pour into a quart bottle and fill up with whisky. Cork well, and always shake before using.

A pleasant dessert can be made by pouring 4 tablespoons of the above into tall glasses, and topping up with whipped cream. It should be served chilled, the top sprinkled with fine, lightly toasted oatmeal which gives it a nutty flavour.

Golfers, alfresco, at the 19th hole, c. 1890

DIET LOAF

A traditional Scots sponge cake which is very light, and not in the least like a loaf!

'But will ye not take another dish of tea, Maister Francie? . . . and a wee bit of the diet-loaf, raised wi' my ain fresh butter, Maister Francie?'
St Ronan's Well, *Sir Walter Scott.*

1 lb. (2 cups) caster sugar
$\frac{1}{2}$ lb. (1 cup) butter
6 large eggs, or 7 small ones
grated peel of 1 lemon

$\frac{1}{2}$ teasp. ground cinnamon
$\frac{3}{4}$ lb. (3 cups) sifted flour
sprinkling of icing (confectioner's) sugar

Cream the butter and sugar, beat the eggs very well, add them to the creamed butter and sugar, and beat together for about 15 minutes, then add the lemon peel very finely grated and the cinnamon. Gradually add the flour, beating well after each amount is added, and until the mixture is very smooth. Line a baking tin with well-greased paper and pour in the sponge. Bake in a moderate oven (375° F.) until pale golden, and well risen, about 35 minutes, but as it is very light, watch that it does not get too brown. Five minutes before it is cooked strew the top with icing sugar, and put back to finish cooking. Let it stand for a few minutes until it curls from the sides slightly, before removing from the tin and cooling on a rack. If preferred, the icing sugar can be omitted and the cake iced when cold.

e new velocipede, West Pans, 1885. Photograph by Mr Aird

SPELDINGS

Speldings are small fish which are members of the cod (Gadus) family. By the Moray and Dornoch Firths they used to be cleaned, split, lightly salted and strung through the eye-balls, then hung up in a cool (not sunny) place to dry, for one or two days. This method is called 'blawn' or wind-blown, and is also done with small whitings or haddocks, but the latter are left unsplit until cooking time; they are called rizzared haddocks.

Roll lightly in flour, then grill lightly on both sides, either over a peat fire or a brander (which is like a girdle, except that it is slotted like a grill) or under a modern griller. Serve hot with a knob of butter on top, and a good sprinkling of freshly ground pepper. Or they can be lightly poached, drained and served with a small jug of melted butter. Oatcakes should be served as well, for they go very well together.

CABBIE-CLAW

In Shetland dialect a young cod is called a kabbilow, *which undoubtedly comes from the French* cabillaud.

1 whole, young codling about 2½ lb.	water
2 tablesp. coarse sea-salt	1 lb. cooked, hot mashed potatoes
1 sprig parsley	parsley and cayenne pepper to garnish
2 teasp. grated horse-radish	

Speldings drying at Cromarty, c. 1890

FOR THE EGG SAUCE[1]

2 tablesp. butter	½ pt. (1 cup) of water the fish is cooked in
2 tablesp. flour	
½ pt. (1 cup) milk	a pinch of nutmeg, salt and pepper
2 hard-boiled eggs	

The fish must be very fresh. Clean it and remove the eyes, split it and then wipe it with a clean cloth. Rub the coarse salt inside and out, and leave it overnight. The next day hang it up in the shade, in a cool, draughty place for 24 hours. Then cover it with boiling water, with the parsley and horse-radish, and simmer very gently until it is cooked (about 25 minutes, depending on size). Lift it out gently, then remove the skin and all the bones and break it roughly with a fork into large pieces. Put it on a hot dish and keep it warm in a slow oven.

MEANWHILE MAKE THE SAUCE: melt the butter, stir in the flour, then gradually add the hot stock and the milk, stirring all the time to keep it smooth. Chop the whites and yolks of the hard-boiled eggs separately, then stir in the whites and seasoning. Pour this over the fish, and garnish the top with the coarsely shredded yolks. Arrange the finely mashed potatoes around the outside, and garnish it all with chopped parsley and a sprinkling of cayenne pepper.
Serves 4.

[1] When served with boiled chicken, the fish stock is replaced with chicken stock.

BANNOCKS OR OATCAKES

Traditional.

The girdle or griddle is one of the oldest cooking utensils, common to all the Celtic countries, from Brittany to Ireland. The word probably comes from the Old French, grédil, *meaning grid-iron, although the hot stones used for baking by the early Gaels were called* greadeal. *It is used for cooking bread, bannocks or scones, and is then sprinkled only with flour before cooking: if a batter is used, the girdle is very slightly greased. In some cottages the girdle is rested on a tripod over the peat embers, not suspended.*

Froissart, the fourteenth-century chronicler, writes that the Scottish soldier always carried a flat plate of metal and a wallet of oatmeal, as part of his equipment. With a little water he could always make himself an oatcake over a wood fire, which contributed to his remarkable stamina.

Oatcakes are very good with fish, especially herrings, either smoked or fresh, with raw onions and butter: also served with soups, buttermilk, or with jam, honey or marmalade for breakfast.

It is easier to make 1 large oatcake at a time and cut it into quarters (or farls) for cooking, as the mixture stiffens if left too long. After cooking they can be stored in a tin, and either lightly toasted, or heated in a slow oven to crisp them. A heavy frying-pan can be used instead of a girdle, or they can be baked in a moderate oven (325° F.) for about 20 minutes. This quantity makes 1 large bannock the size of a dinner plate (or 4 to 8 small ones). The girdle must be heated before baking.

4 oz. (⅔ cup) medium oatmeal	additional oatmeal for the kneading
2 teasp. melted fat (bacon dripping is good)	a pinch of salt
a pinch of bicarbonate of soda	about ¼ cup hot water

Mix the oatmeal with the salt and bicarbonate of soda in a basin, then make a well in the middle and pour in the melted fat. Stir around, then add enough water to make a stiff paste. Scatter a board or table thickly with oatmeal, turn out the mixture and roll into a ball. Knead well with the hands covered in oatmeal to prevent sticking. Press down a little and keep the edges as regular as possible. Then roll out to ¼-in. thickness, and shape by putting a dinner plate on top and cutting round the edges. Sprinkle finally with a little meal, then cut into quarters or less. Place on the warmed girdle, or pan, and cook until the edges curl slightly. In Scotland they were finished on a toasting stone, but a medium hot grill to crisp the other side is adequate. Mix another bannock whilst the oatcakes are 'finishing'.

Warming up the girdle, Isle of Barra

POTTED TROUT

From the manuscript book of Lady Theodora Forbes, 1867–1953.

These fish will keep for some time in a cold place, if completely covered by the melted butter.

12 trout	¼ pt. (½ cup) wine vinegar
1 lb. butter	salt and pepper
a pinch each of mace, nutmeg, ground clove	

Scale and clean the trout well. Wash them over with a little wine vinegar, and slit them down the back. Remove the backbone, and sprinkle with salt and pepper, both inside and out, then leave for several hours to absorb. Put them head to tail in an ovenproof dish with a liberal nut of butter on each one, using about half the quantity given. Cover, and bake them for ¾ hour in a slow to moderate oven (300°–325° F.). Take them out of the liquid, carefully, and put into a clean dish. When cold, cover them completely with the remainder of the butter which has been just heated up with the mace, nutmeg, and clove. Serve cold.

This recipe can also be used for herrings.

BOILED GIGOT OF MUTTON OR LAMB

Traditionally boiled in water to cover, with carrots and turnips, in Scotland, but the following recipe from Mrs Young of The Hotel, Portsonachan, Dalmally, Argyll, is excellent, especially for older meat. Gigot is the word used for a leg of mutton, as in France; an inheritance from the days of the 'Auld Alliance'.

1 leg mutton or lamb about 4–5 lb.
2 large onions
2 carrots
1 sprig rosemary
1 bay leaf
6 black peppercorns
a sprig parsley, and thyme
milk to cover
salt

FOR CAPER SAUCE
2 tablesp. flour
2 tablesp. butter
3 tablesp. capers and a little of the juice
1½ pt. (3 cups) of the lamb stock
salt and pepper to taste

Remove any surplus fat from the meat, place in a deep saucepan and pour in milk to come three-quarters of the way up. Put in the sliced onions, carrots, herbs, and season to taste. Cover and bring gently to the boil, then simmer very gently for 2 to 3 hours or until the meat is tender. Now take out the meat and keep hot. Skim the fat from the milk and strain off about 1½ pt. for the sauce.

TO MAKE THE SAUCE
Melt the butter, stir in the flour, and cook for 1 minute. Add the warm milk stock, stirring all the time to prevent lumps. Add the capers and the juice (about 1 tablespoon) and stir again until well mixed and creamy. Carve the lamb on a hot ashet (dish), cover with sauce and surround with small boiled potatoes sprinkled with parsley, carrots cooked with a pinch of sugar and sprinkled with chopped mint.

A stop for refreshment, near Edinburgh, 1885. Photograph by Mr Aird

Rob Roy, *pleasure steamer, Loch Katrine, the Trossachs, 189*

SALMON FRITTERS

½ lb. (approx. 2 cups) cold, boiled, boned, flaked salmon
2 heaped tablesp. flour
2 eggs
¼ pt. (½ cup) cream or top of the milk
salt and cayenne pepper
oil for frying

FOR THE SAUCE
4 oz. (½ cup) melted butter
2 tablesp. cream
2 teasp. flour
2 teasp. soy sauce
2 teasp. mushroom ketchup

Flake the boned and skinned fish, add the flour, the beaten eggs and enough milk or cream to make the mixture a soft consistency like a sponge dough. Season to taste. Have the oil very hot, and drop in tablespoons of the mixture, fry until golden brown on both sides, then drain on paper. Keep warm.

To make the sauce, mix the cream with the flour and add to the melted butter, heating it and stirring all the time. When it has thickened slightly add the soy sauce and mushroom ketchup, mixing them well through the sauce.

Serves 3 to 4.

These fritters can be made with almost any white fish, or shellfish such as lobster or crab.

DROP OR DROPPED SCONES

Traditionally cooked on a girdle (see page 102), but they can be successfully made in a heavy frying-pan, or the covered-in top of an electric grill. 'Scone' comes from the Gaelic sgonn, and rhymes with gone. Some recipes use baking powder, but personally I prefer the following method.

1 lb. (4 cups) self-raising flour
2 tablesp. light golden syrup or corn syrup (this gives the scones a nice smooth surface)
½ teasp. salt

½ pint (1 cup) approx. milk or buttermilk
3 oz. (3 heaped tablesp.) sugar
2 eggs

Put the flour, sugar, salt and warmed syrup into the mixing bowl, then add the milk and beaten eggs until the mixture forms a thick dropping consistency like a thick cream. Heat up the girdle or the pan, and very lightly grease it. Drop by tablespoons in rounds, seeing that they do not overlap and are even (if you are unused to making them, it is better to do them singly). Turn over when little bubbles appear on top and the bottom is golden brown, then cook the other side. Cool in a clean tea-towel or napkin, keeping them wrapped unless they are to be eaten hot from the pan. Serve them warm or cold with butter, heather honey or jam. They will keep for some time in a tin, and can be heated up by putting them either in a warm oven or under a slow grill.

Makes about 24 scones.

Fish-smoking, and clothes drying, by the shores of the Moray Firth, c. *1890*

CULLEN SKINK

Traditional to the Moray Firth. Skink comes from the Gaelic, and originally meant 'essence'; nowadays it means a stew-soup.

1 large smoked haddock, preferably Finnan, about 2 lb.
1 medium sliced onion
1½ pt. (3 cups) milk

2 tablesp. butter
8 oz. (2 cups) approx. cooked mashed potato
salt and pepper

Put the haddock in a shallow pan, skin side down, with just enough cold water to cover it, bring to the boil, then simmer for 4 minutes. Turn the fish, and with a small slice take off the skin, add the sliced onion, cover, and simmer very gently for about 10 minutes. Take the fish out and remove all the bones, then put them back in the stock and simmer again for about 20 minutes, then strain. Put the stock and the milk in a saucepan, add the filleted fish, bring to boiling-point, then add enough mashed potato to make it creamy and the consistency you like. Add the butter in very small pieces, and season to taste. The last of the butter added should hardly melt, but run in little yellow rivulets through the soup-stew. Serve with triangles of dry toast. Some cooks add a little cream before serving, but it is neither traditional nor, in my opinion, necessary.

Serves 3 to 4.

On the grouse moor, Edinglasse, Aberdeenshire, 189

BREAD SAUCE

This is a Scots invention, and always served with roasted poultry or feathered game. An early form is given in Mrs Cleland's book, A New and Easy Method of Cookery, 1759, for serving with ducks, partridges and moor-fowl. Bread is boiled in water with a blade of mace, an onion stuffed with cloves, a good piece of butter and a little salt. She adds '. . you may put a little white wine and ketchup in it'.

heaped tablesp. white bread-crumbs	4 peppercorns
medium onion	¾ pt. (1½ cups) milk
cloves	1 teasp. butter
pinch of mace	2 tablesp. cream
	salt and pepper

Stick the cloves into the onion and put into a saucepan with the milk, mace and peppercorns. Bring to the boil, then draw aside and let it infuse for about ½ hour. Strain the milk into another saucepan and add the breadcrumbs. Stir until it is boiling and quite thick. Season to taste and finally stir in the butter and cream. Do not reboil after this, and serve hot.

Makes approximately 2 cups.

ROASTIT BUBBLY-JOCK

Probably gets its name from the gobbling voice of the live turkey. Recipe of Mrs Buchanan, 1891.

1 hen turkey, about 12 lb.	FOR THE STUFFING
1 lb. sausage-meat	4 oz. (1 cup) breadcrumbs
5 tablesp. good poultry dripping	6 oysters fresh or canned
2 oz. melted butter	8 large peeled chestnuts
1 tablesp. redcurrant or cranberry jelly	1 small chopped celery heart
	¼ pt. (½ cup) milk
salt and pepper	chopped raw turkey liver
1 pt. (2 cups) giblet stock	1 teasp. chopped parsley

To make the stuffing, soak the breadcrumbs in the milk and then combine all the other ingredients, and stuff well into the body of the bird, securing with a skewer. Put the sausage-meat into the crop opening and skewer, too. Put the bird in the roasting tin and brush all over with the melted butter, and put the dripping around, cover with foil and roast in a slow to moderate oven (300° F.) for 20–25 minutes to the pound. Baste about half-way through cooking time, and add salt and pepper. Remove paper 15 minutes before it is cooked and baste again, then remove bird to a warmed dish. Pour off excess fat from the pan, add the giblet stock and redcurrant jelly. Adjust seasoning, and boil up rapidly on top of the stove to reduce. Serve sauce separately.

SHORTBREAD

'To beat the Edinburgh baker, you must go – not to London, but – to Paris or Vienna.'

        Old World Scotland, T. F. Henderson, 1893.

'If every Frenchwoman is born with a wooden spoon in her hand, every Scotswoman is born with a rolling-pin under her arm.'

        The Scots Kitchen, F. Marian McNeill.

Eaten all the year round but especially at Christmas and the New Year, this delicious cake, which is quite unlike any other, is made from only the finest materials. Butter is essential, it is pointless to attempt it with margarine. Originally made with fine oatmeal, it is now made with sifted flour, sometimes with a small proportion (2 oz. to 14 oz. flour) of rice flour. On festive occasions it can be decorated with fine strips of orange or lemon peel and small sugared almonds. In the Shetland and Orkney Islands it is called the Bride's Bonn, and has a small proportion (about 2 teaspoons) of caraway seeds added. The edges are traditionally 'notched' by pinching with the finger and thumb, and this is thought to symbolize the sun's rays, from the early days of sun-worship.

    The following recipe was given to me by Sheena Anderson, and although it does not use rice flour, I can vouch for its excellence.

1 lb. (4 cups) plain flour	½ lb. (1 cup) caster sugar
1 lb. (4 cups) self-raising flour	½ teasp. salt
1 lb. (2 cups) butter	

Cream the butter and sugar together, then work in the sieved flours and salt, very lightly until the mixture resembles short-crust pastry. Do not knead it, for that toughens it. Turn out on to a lightly floured board or table, and press with the hand into one or two large rounds. Do not roll, for this also toughens it. Put on to an ungreased baking sheet, pinch the edges with finger and thumb and prick all over with a fork. Bake in a slow to moderate oven (250° F. to 275° F.) for about 1 hour. Leave to cool before turning out on to a rack.

TWEED KETTLE

Scotch salmon is renowned for its excellence, and the simpler ways of cooking it preserve the delicate flavour. Smoked salmon should be served with only a squeeze of lemon, a little red pepper, and home-made brown bread and butter. As recently as 1820 salmon were seen in the Clyde near Jamaica Bridge.

Tweed Kettle or Salmon Hash is a nineteenth-century Edinburgh speciality.

3 lb. fresh salmon (the tail-end is best)	½ pt. (1 cup) water from fish
2 chopped shallots *or*	½ pt. (1 cup) white wine
2 tablesp. chopped chives	a pinch of ground mace
salt and freshly milled pepper	2 tablesp. chopped parsley

Put the fish into a kettle and cover with water, then bring to the boil and simmer for 5 minutes only. Remove from the stock but reserve it. Take all the skin from the fish, also the bones, and cut it int cubes about 2 in. across, season with salt, pepper and mace, the put back into a saucepan with 1 cup of the fish stock, the wine, an chives. Cover, and simmer very slowly for about 25 minutes. Ad the chopped parsley before serving either hot or cold.

Serves 6.

POTTED SALMON

Recipe from a picnic luncheon at Fas-na-darroch, Aberdeenshire, 187℅

Mix 2 cups cold, boneless salmon with 3 pounded anchovies or tablespoon anchovy paste, ¼ lb. (½ cup) butter, a pinch of mace, sa and cayenne pepper. Pound it well, and press into a dish. Cove with melted butter, chill, and serve with rolls or toast.

Serves 4 to 6.

Benmore *leaving the Broomielaw on the Clyde, Glasgow, c. 1890. Photograph by George Washington Wilson*
The Broomielaw is so called from the days when this part of the river bank was clad in 'bonny yellow broom'.)

Self-portrait of Mr Aird, 1885, aged thirty-nine years, photographe
of plates on pages 11, 67, 98, 107

INDEX